Matthew, Tell Me About Heaven

A Firsthand Description of the Afterlife

A Matthew Book with Suzanne Ward

Readers' Comments

I was quite amazed at the details that your son went into to describe the afterlife. I always imagined the afterlife as sort of an emotionless, timeless, nothingness...I guess I was wrong!

—**Brian Lohman**, Illinois

I do not think I can do justice with mere words to the feelings this message inspired. After I started reading, it was difficult to put the book down to do the necessary things. It was a most glorious meal for the spirit.

—**Eve Howard**, Indiana

Matthew, Tell Me About Heaven brought me tears of joy, moments of elation and a profound new "innerstanding" of what life on Earth is all about and what happens to us after we die. This opening of the Veil and revelation of what had been hidden to mankind for so long has the power to change the world beyond our wildest imaginings.

This is not about religion or another new age fad. This is about the most vital awareness that can emerge only when we allow our divine Self to shine through, learning as we go that there is so much more to life than what our collective cultural trance has allowed us to grasp so far.

Jean Hudon, author of *The Immortal Child*, Quebec

I find *Matthew, Tell Me About Heaven* inspirational, enlightening and soothing. It gives me even more hope and understanding of what is to become of us, and our spiritual evolution's important role in our lives.

—**Nahla Rifa**, Amman, Jordan

I really want to THANK YOU *again* so much for these books. What Joy!! They confirm and confirm and confirm other channeled info about the many subjects covered in Matthew's books. Truly great info and confirmations. Truth, when known, gives such joy.

—**Vivien R.**, California

For a great many people awash in uncertainty and confusion, feeling the unmistakable stirrings of their own dormant Godness rousing from a lifelong torpor, the book that could unlock the Gates of Heaven, metaphorically and literally, might just be *Matthew, Tell Me About Heaven.* It is an invaluable "tour guide" for the many who are still terrified of death and what awaits them beyond this mortal vale. Few books I have read demystify the process so comfortably and accessibly.

—**Randy Mitchell**, North Carolina

It isn't very often that I read something so moving, compelling, and thought provoking that I literally could not put it down. As I start to embrace my own life's purpose, I find it so helpful to have stories and material such as this to get me through those times when I get frustrated or I just don't think I can do it. Your books give me much to think about during those times and gently help my perspective drift back towards the spiritual and the positive.

—**Shane Magee**, California

Matthew, Tell Me About Heaven is the missing link to many of our questions on life before now and the hereafter. We read, learned and heard bits and pieces here and there but never were quite able to fit it all together. This book reveals the information that gels it all, fitting the missing pieces of the jigsaw puzzle into a big picture of what is meant to be understood. Truth and knowledge seekers of the Light will resonate with profound information that triggers remembrance in the deep-seated recesses of our subconscious mind. This book will certainly comfort millions.

—**Chooi-Chin Goh**, United Kingdom

Thank you so much for sharing these wonderful two books. With growing enthusiasm I read them both during the past 10 days and believe you helped me take a number of steps on my bridge towards spiritual awakening.

—**Bernd Nurnberger**, Yokohama, Japan

Matthew, Tell Me About Heaven

ISBN 0-9717875-1-4

Library of Congress 2002090382

This book was printed in the United States of America
Second Printing 2003

MATTHEW BOOKS
P.O. Box 1043
Camas, Washington 98607

www.matthewbooks.com
suzy@matthewbooks.com

CONTENTS

FOREWORD

All of us who have experienced the death of someone paramount and precious in our lives know that the loss forever changes who we were. In this, our grief is similar, but for each aching heart there also is a unique story of love.

This is much more than my story. It *is* about love—personal *and* divine—but more, it is evidence that when our beloved people leave this world, they live in another body in a wondrous realm of amazing activity and diversity. Our religions hold that there is an "afterlife" in the "next world" in accordance with how life is lived in this one. That is so, but their impressions about that world have misconceptions because it is concluded that once there, no one can give us a report. And that is *not* so!

We *can* know—we are *meant* to know—about that realm we call Heaven and whose proper name, my son Matthew told me, is Nirvana. We can envision our beloved people there, where many aspects are surprisingly similar to life here. But Heaven offers far more love and enlightenment, fairness and kindness, and health in mind, body and spirit than life on Earth does. From these disclosures about life in Heaven we will understand the purpose of our lives here and learn how to prepare for moving onward. And we can rejoice in knowing that love bonds are more than memories and eternal life is more than nebulous imaginings!

EDITOR'S NOTE

Almost always Matthew uses masculine pronouns to denote both male and female. As he requested of me, *"Please accept this as intended, only for ease of my speaking and your hearing and NEVER as a suggestion of male priority in any respect."*

Although almost all phraseology attributed to Matthew is his verbatim, I did eliminate redundancy and verbosity. Also I rearranged some of his statements for smoother flow of the information, amended wording to make natural transitions when integrating related material from different transmissions, and devised some questions or comments to achieve the most logical order for the chapters.

Some information in PART II will be more easily understood with PART I as context, so starting at the beginning is recommended. Insofar as possible, the chapters in PART II are arranged to introduce life in Heaven as it might unfold to you or me. Even though all are designed to make sense alone, some passages require an understanding of information in previous chapters, and reading them in order also is recommended. Reading the glossary before continuing could be helpful, too.

PART I

MATTHEW

BONDS BETWEEN SOULS

Late afternoon April 17, 1980, 17-year-old Matthew was driving home after a full day's work at his father's farm in Panama. The men who saw him thrown from his Jeep after it veered off the road and crashed in a rocky field said there was no apparent reason for the accident. The driver wasn't speeding. There was no other traffic, weather and visibility were optimum, the road was in good condition. Yet, there was the crash, and my son died in the arms of his rescuers.

Almost fourteen years later:

SUZANNE: Matthew, what caused the crash?

MATTHEW: It's what the family finally concluded, that I simply dozed off. At least that's the reason the Jeep went off the road. I know some of you thought if only I'd been listening to the radio, it would have kept me awake. No, Mother, that wouldn't have changed anything. It was my soul contract. My time had come, and if I hadn't been fatally injured when I wrecked the Jeep, I would have left some other way at that same time of my life.

S: The doctor said your injuries were so massive that you couldn't have survived even with immediate medical help. But all of the mediums I went to told me you felt no pain because your spirit left your body prior to the crash and you witnessed it from above. How could both be true?

MATTHEW: The mediums told you what I told them, and hearing that did comfort you, didn't it? That's what I intended. But it wasn't totally accurate for me to say there was no pain, because my body did feel the impact.

It *is* true that my *soul* was released from my body prior to that moment, so there wasn't trauma to my entire being. If my soul had stayed within my body then, my psyche would have been severely traumatized prior to my arrival here. Avoiding that kind of trauma is one form of divine grace. It permits easier and faster healing and adjustment here, without the need for the prolonged, intricate treatment required to restore a damaged psyche to full functioning ability. So I did arrive in good condition psychically.

S: Since your intent was to comfort me, why did you wait nine months to contact me, in my first dream about you after you died? The medium I talked with shortly after the crash said you weren't ready to communicate with me. Her exact words were, "He is in deep rest and reevaluating his decision to exit," and she said you would give me an unmistakable sign when you were ready. I interpreted my dream as that sign.

MATTHEW: You were right about the dream being my sign to you, but that medium could just as well have said I was "de-pressed." Mother, I encountered difficulty I wasn't expecting, and my first several months here were totally unproductive, a very emotionally stressful time.

I want you to know that adjustment here does NOT have to be that way! Like every other soul who arrives, I was greeted lovingly and offered every possible assistance and solace during those months. But nothing then could relieve my preoccupation with the family's reaction to my leaving Earth life. I hadn't counted on regretting or doubting the wisdom of our pre-birth agreement to let me leave at that young age. But when we made that agreement, we hadn't anticipated the actual intensity and duration of family grief.

In this realm we feel what our beloved souls on Earth are feeling. I never wished to return, but your pain kept me closely bound to all of you during those early months. I was just as paralyzed by it as you were until I was able to fully accept my leaving in accordance with our agreement and shake myself loose from the family's grief.

S: I don't know anything about those "family agreements" you're talking about, and I'm sorry we affected you the way we did. But OF COURSE we felt grief, Matthew! Just how did you expect us to react to losing you?!

MATTHEW: Mother, dear, I'm *not* criticizing your feelings. I'm only explaining my beginning here. It was never a case of what *I* expected, it was that everyone's pain was far greater than *any* of us expected when we made the agreement.

S: How could any agreement be so unthinkably cruel that it wouldn't consider that?

MATTHEW: A pre-birth agreement is *never* a punishment or an impersonal levy. Our agreement was made by *all of us* at soul level. We had shared lifetimes before, and we had gained emotional strength during those experiences. We chose each other to be a family because every one of us would be given situations and conditions we needed for advancing our spiritual growth. Spiritual growth is what life on Earth is all about.

At the time of our soul level discussions, all of us felt that my early departure would be handled in a healthful way that would contribute to everyone's lifetime missions. That isn't what happened, though. The grieving was not healthful.

S: *What is "healthful" grieving?*

MATTHEW: It's allowing spiritual strength to let you release the beloved person to begin his new life. When you continue to agonize over what you call the death, or loss, of that person, his soul is bound to you. Our bonds in grief are as strong as our bonds in love, and both have powerful effects on us here. The negatively-charged energy of prolonged grief prevents our moving forward in soul evolvement, whereas the positive energy of love illuminates our spiritual pathway and accelerates our growth.

Of course you miss the physical closeness! When there is love, there's no way to avoid that natural sorrow at the parting. But if you will accept it, you will be given spiritual strength in the shared love instead of the crippling effects of shared grief. And you will know that your healthful grieving is helping us as well.

S: *If your bonds with us stay so strong, Matthew, how can you ever have a normal or independent life there?*

MATTHEW: Mother, it's no different from loving people in Earth lifetimes and still enjoying other aspects of life. When I finally started moving ahead here, it was because I was free of grief, NOT because I stopped loving you all! Our love bonds are as strong as ever!

As for my life here—once I let it get underway—it has been WONDERFUL! I have good friends and especially beloved souls. My work is immensely gratifying. I enjoy sports just as I used to and many other leisure time activities, and I study, I travel. Now I have this communion with you, just as the mediums told you we would. So, wouldn't you say that this life is "normal and independent"? I'd say so!

S: *Yes, dear, it does sound like a full life, a good life, and*

naturally I'm happy about that. But we still miss you, Mat-
thew. Why did your death at such a young age have to be a
part of our family's agreement? I can't believe I ever agreed
to that.

MATTHEW: You did, Mother, and nothing that isn't
necessary for *everyone's* experiencing would ever be part of
the family's agreement. For the moment, please let's just
leave it at that.

OUR FAMILY

From the beginning, Matthew's life was a celebration of independence. He made that known in the moment I first held him, and I respected it throughout his years on Earth. The third of my four children, he was born when Eric was four and Betsy, almost three. The older children were so fulfilled by each other that only occasionally did they show interest in their little brother. So for almost two years Matthew and I were mostly alone except for our gentle old spaniel Freckles, with whom he had the same endearing closeness he had with our dogs who came afterwards.

Until he started to talk, shortly before his second birthday and two months after Michael was born, Matthew was uncommonly serious and observant. I talked to him a great deal, but he listened only in silence. His father thought he was retarded, but I knew better. When I would tell him we must treat all animals and each other kindly or that we could see God everywhere around us, he appeared to be absorbing my words as if his life depended upon his repeating them all. When my topics and tone were lighthearted, his disarming smile tilted upward and his gray eyes sparkled, as if he was keeping a mischievous secret. I was not surprised that once Matthew became vocal, he spoke plainly in complete sentences, and soon he was giving opinions—sometimes startlingly mature and wise—on any subject to whoever would listen.

When Matthew was three we moved from Miami to the Republic of Panama. It was a corporate move that took the children's father back to his birthplace and provided a large, attentive extended family and the multicultural environment that influenced subsequent choices in our lives. In his new surroundings, Matthew flourished in his bilingual blend of vibrant activity, introspection and imagination. His first-grade teacher called me about her annoyance that he turned the numbers on his test papers into flowers. Those little embellishments grew into surreal vistas, spaceships and strange-appearing beings on art pads and interspersed with studies in his high school notebooks.

Until his last hour on Earth, Matthew made life overflow for him. He and Eric would discover or invent adventure. They mastered tough maneuvers on skateboards, surfboards and motocross bikes, and Matthew played basketball, tennis and soccer. Younger Michael wasn't his brothers' equal in sports, but better yet, he was the third Ward boy. By the time all were teenagers, the trio had become an asset to any party, trustworthy allies and formidable competition.

Also by that time, for several years the children had been traveling back and forth between their father's home in Panama and wherever I was in the States. Divorce had ended the family and geographic stability of their lives. Two years after the divorce, the same month Matthew turned ten, the children and I moved from Panama to Virginia, near Washington, DC, the first of my several work-related moves.

The children were having to grow up in a hurry. Eric got a driver's license early on a family hardship basis, Betsy was self-appointed assistant mother and counselor to her brothers, Matthew became a savvy price comparison shopper and innovative cook, Michael wrote menus and grocery lists. All had pride in our home, wherever it was. They enthusiastically participated in refurbishing and decor and, perhaps less eagerly, handled housekeeping chores.

For a sense of roots, since the children had been born in Miami, they became avid fans of the Dolphins.

Even without the presence of their father, the children and I were a sound family, solidified in spirit. Nevertheless, those migratory years of our lives presented difficult challenges for all of us, and eventually I was alone. Eric moved back to Panama for his senior year and later, combined working and university studies. The next year Betsy enrolled in Virginia Tech. To avoid more disruption due to my moves, Matthew and Michael went to a boarding school in Florida near my mother and other family, and later they, too, went back to Panama to complete high school.

Being able to envision the children in their surroundings during our geographic separations was vital to my sense of motherhood. I had lived in or visited the places where each of them was, so I was familiar with their environments and companions. I could imagine them studying and socializing; surfing, cycling and rapping; working at their various jobs; sitting at their father's and stepmother's dining table. However far away my children were, with myriad mental pictures of them I was still an onlooker of sorts, if not a participant in their daily activities. Inextricably interwoven with bonds of love, that perspective let me feel close to them during the many periods when we were apart.

On April 16, 1980, Matthew was in Panama. He had graduated a semester early and was working on his father's spice farm until coming to live with me in Philadelphia, where I had moved less than four months before. Matthew's letters were mostly enthusiastic reports about the responsibilities his father had entrusted to him, and which were delaying his departure several weeks beyond his original schedule. Later I would learn that he and Betsy had made a new plan, to surprise me on Mother's Day weekend, but on this night of Matthew's call with belated birthday wishes, I was chiding him about having forgotten his poor old mom.

He said, *"I think of you every day and I love you every day, and I always will. Don't ever forget that."*

The next night Matthew's father called to tell me our son was dead.

FACING OUR LOSS

In the hours before my flight I couldn't assimilate that news about Matthew. It wasn't real that suddenly he could be gone, and the familiar images I had of him when we were apart no longer would fit. I simply could not *not* have any frame of reference at all for him! I thought of words, "Matthew is with God," but that was not comforting—I was not ready for my son to do that! Matthew's and my world would be shattered if I accepted that! I needed to feel connected with him just the same as when we'd been separated before, with my storehouse of images. But they had become a frantic kaleidoscope and I couldn't see him clearly in my mind any longer.

When Betsy and I met in Miami to travel together to Panama, she told me, "You've lost a son. I've lost a son and a brother." Her years as assistant mother were etched so strongly in her mind and heart that I could believe, if not feel, her double loss. My heart ached for my daughter, who had had to become a woman so young, yet I could do nothing to fill that suddenly desolate space in her life, not then, not ever.

That night, when the whole family was looking at Matthew's senior class pictures a cousin had brought from the photographer, we saw that Matthew's eyes were almost mystical, as if he were seeing something deeply beyond our knowing. Betsy was the only one who knew he wanted to be cremated when he died. He had told her that the previous summer, after talking about the book he had just read, *Life After Life*. She remembered what he had said then: *"What comes after life on Earth has to be the greatest adventure of all!"* Could he have known that his adventure would begin only seven months later?

Eric told us he refused to believe what he had heard about Matthew. Instead of going to the morgue in accordance with the message he had received, he drove for an hour until he reached that isolated place in the country where he saw the Jeep, ominously still in the rocky field. He ran to the bashed vehicle, kicked it again and again and screamed at it like a madman, he said, until finally he was forced to think the unthinkable. My oldest child seemed in that moment not the industrious businessman he was becoming, but a brokenhearted little boy helpless to change what he couldn't accept.

Michael and I were in the room he and Matthew had shared. While Michael had seen his family in reactions from hysteria to quiet tears, he seemed to be caught in silence. I thought that talking about Matthew would help him open up and I spoke about the two of them in that room, the many talks they must have had there. Michael blurted out, "It should have been me who died instead of Matthew, so everybody wouldn't feel so terrible." How could I hurt any more than that, hearing my youngest child tell me he thought his life didn't matter to the rest of us as much as his brother's did? "Michael, sweetheart, don't you know that if you had died, Matthew and I would be here talking about you, missing you, and feeling the very same way you and I are?"

I could see the pain of my children and I hurt dreadfully for them, but some level of my mind still was protecting me from the reality of Matthew's death, as if I alone knew his absence among us was only temporary. Even the next morning as I stood beside his body in the morgue, I felt a strange sense of relief—my Matthew was not in that body. Later, some of us were practicing hymns and "Bless the Beasts and the Children" for the next day's memorial service, when Eric came home and cried out, "How can you sing when he's being cremated?" Because the cremation wasn't real for me, either, but having good music at a service for Matthew was. As I was helping the rest of the family arrange in the church the many flowering plants and trees, I felt gladdened by all those gifts for my boy, who would nurture them just as he had our flowers at home and, so recently, spice seedlings at his father's farm.

Those and the other distortions of my psyche that softened my first days continued until the night after the service. The rest of the family were sleeping when it hit me: ***Matthew was gone forever.***

It came with such a blow that I rushed to the balcony so I wouldn't disturb anyone, and I sobbed so profoundly that my body became weak and my mind became clear. I had gone from delusion to consummate agony to an uncommonly peaceful acceptance in half an hour or so, and to my surprise, I was hungry. Only then did I realize that I hadn't eaten during my three days in Panama.

I took a plate of cold snacks to the dining room and sat facing the line of lights in the bay, where ships were waiting their turn to transit the canal. I was observing this panorama along with the lights of the city and thinking about happy times with Matthew. In the lovely hilltop condo belonging to my former husband and his wife, where Matthew had so recently been, I was feeling unusually serene.

I was smiling, remembering my fearless son climbing a waterfall in the rain forest, when the large, open balcony doorway suddenly filled with a translucent image of Matthew's head. His gray eyes were sparkling, his mischievous grin was right there, and his skin coloring, evanescent though the image was, was his wholesome tan. The joy I felt was unlike any other moment. I could feel the love emanating from Matthew's image and coming into me and the motion of my love flowing to him. Our all-encompassing love circle continued for perhaps a minute before the vision, which had so abruptly appeared, started slowly receding, as if reluctant to leave. After the last faint vision faded entirely, the love bond remained as strong as it had been throughout that magical, joy-filled spiritual reunion.

We, Matthew's family, began to resume our lives without him. Perhaps we returned to the same pathway, but with a different step or heartbeat. Or perhaps we started, unwittingly, on a completely different pathway. Who can know how much our lives since then have been influenced by the loss of Matthew's involvement?

I don't know how I would have dealt with his death over the years if I had remained afterwards in Panama, a country for which I still have great fondness, surrounded by family and friends. Maybe I wouldn't have fared there any better than anywhere else, because the facts were unchangeable. Never again could I hug my son, or laugh with him. I'd never see him grow into a man, a husband, a father.

And so I came back to a city of strangers and a job where I was expected to function responsibly, make sound decisions, and help my staff and colleagues feel comfortable around me. Eerily for the college administration, at the same time Matthew died three other parents lost children, too. The president's son, the same age as Matthew, had died in a car crash. A woman who became pregnant for the first time after 20 years of trying to have a baby, had a stillborn girl. Another woman was mourning the death of her 33-year-old daughter, a mother herself, who was recovering well from simple surgery and abruptly died.

Only once did they and I speak about our respective losses. The mother of the infant said that most people told her it was a blessing her baby had not lived at all because she couldn't miss what she had never known. She told me no one could know the pain she felt about her baby, who meant more to her than anything else in this world. She said, "I wish I could have had her for 17 years, like you had your boy."

After the president and I talked about the similarity of our sons' lives and deaths, he took my hand, and for a moment we wept together before he silently left my office.

The grandmother told me it wasn't any easier or any harder for her just because she had her daughter twice as long as I'd had my son. It was a heartache for her to see the bewilderment of her young grandchild and the suffering of her son-in-law. She said that when our children die even before our parents do, that's such a wrong order of life. "Why does God let these things happen?" she asked me.

None of the three parents ever again sought me, nor I them, for some special moment of empathy. Maybe they were learning, as I was, that grief is an intensely painful private journey.

A cousin especially dear to Betsy and me was coming to spend Mother's Day weekend with us. Instead, a few days before that, he died of a heart attack and my daughter and I met in Cleveland to attend the second family funeral within three weeks. But we cried for Matthew, not Richard, because we had no space for more sorrow.

My broken life was fortified by work. I was fortunate in having a staff of sensitive young people who also were good writers and meticulous copy editors. In our first meeting after my return, one told of an incident during my absence, when she "died laughing." I broke the sudden silence by assuring them that the expression was natural, it didn't hurt. And that was so, because I didn't associate it with Matthew. But I did associate with him billboard ads for Pepsi, smiling faces, airlines and "pop" radio stations, and it was in my half-hour drives to and from the college that I allowed myself to cry.

Weeknights I stayed at my office until ten o'clock, often later, and on weekends I had a briefcase filled with manuscripts to read and edit, reports to complete and correspondence to answer. These were a reliable crutch when I was alone, requiring a level of concentration that could screen out feelings, and I stopped only when I fell asleep on the work at hand. My first weeks passed in that mechanical sphere with only brief and infrequent moments of allowing the Whole Truth to overwhelm me.

Twice, when agony was so consuming I felt it was eating me alive, I made middle-of-the-night calls, not to family or dear friends, but unlikely choices. When I identified myself to the first, he told me nothing could be so important that it couldn't have waited until morning. The other, a recent acquaintance whose daughter had died the previous year, was indifferent to whether or not I could now empathize with his grief. A friend who knew Matthew well called, and after I told him, he said, "I don't want to hear this, it couldn't have happened."

In June, looking gaunt and sober and with his leg in a cast, Michael came with his father for Betsy's graduation, and Michael came back with me to Philadelphia for the summer, as planned. He hobbled around the college stuffing envelopes until he could start the gardening he'd been hired to do, unaware that his salary was siphoned from mine. Occasionally we accepted invitations from people who meant to be thoughtful but hadn't an iota of understanding how painful it was for me to try to act cheerful. Michael seemed more at ease on those occasions than I, and he enjoyed his job and the compliments that the large courtyard had never looked better.

Betsy took a break in her post-grad work for the week my sister-in-law was with me while her teen-aged son was having orthopedic surgery. I saw him lying motionless, still under the anesthesia, on those pristine white sheets and thought of Matthew in the morgue while I comforted Marlene in her anxiety about the intricate operation's out-come. When my landlord evicted me for having more people in the apartment than the three residents I'd stipulated in the contract, the judge threw out the case and told him he was heartless, but I said I'd move as soon as I could anyway.

Thus, in many respects, my resumed pathway did con-tinue publicly as life does, but privately there was some se-riously compromised thinking. Since I couldn't undo what had happened to Matthew, I believed that the only way I could ever feel alive again was to join him, and I prayed that I would. That prayer provided me with hope, or maybe only the motivation to do something besides curl into a ball until I could join my son. If I worked hard, my prayer would be answered. If I didn't try diligently, then I wasn't worthy of being with Matthew. It never occurred to me that work-ing long and conscientiously was nothing new. It was the backbone of the "work ethic" my father's life had exempli-fied, and from my first job onward had been mine, too. Sim-ply, I had attached a new reward to it.

That wasn't the only example of my impaired think-ing, but because of its semi-sensible basis in productive func-tioning, it may have been my greatest ally. If there is a way to deal with the death of a child that encompasses sound judgment, I never was in touch with it, and I made some major foolish decisions that brought a series of problems and misery for the next few years. For instance, knowing that funding for the journal I was editing very likely would be switched to medical education programs and I would be out of a job, still I bought a house rather than deal with any landlord again. The consequences of such impetuosity just weren't real to me.

What *was* real was the dark night silence, when conversational thoughts of Matthew sustained our mother-son relationship:

Honey, exactly where is Heaven? Of course that's where you are, isn't it, never mind what you used to say about preferring hell-raising!

Do you have a real body or are you just floating around invisibly, doing God only knows what? Mash, are you an angel now?

I guess you must be happy, dear. I want you to be! That's the idea, isn't it, that Heaven's a happy place?

I hope there are flowers for you. You'd miss them if there aren't any. But there must be, because Heaven is supposed to be beautiful and I don't see how it could be without flowers.

Have you seen Grandpa? Who else is there? How many souls are there altogether? Have you found out yet how it's decided who goes there and who doesn't?

Hey, since you have so much experience being bossy, maybe you can be assistant to St. Peter, or whoever is in charge. Maybe you already are!

Who takes care of the babies who die? Remember when you asked to hold Sandy's newborn baby boy? You did it so confidently, you surprised us all. It's so unfair that you never had a chance to have your own family. Maybe it's because fewer people would miss you all the rest of their lives.

Does Heaven have colors like Earth, like our blue skies and green hills and our red sunsets and pink or yellow blossoms on bushes? Or is everything white? Is there anything we'd recognize—scenery, animals—or only people?

Do you talk to each other or is everything quiet, sort of dream-like? Don't tell me you have that awful music of yours up there! Is my music there? If not, I'm not going. Well, I will go, but I hope you'll talk with Peter or whoever and see what you can do about getting some symphonies before I get there.

How does God keep track of us all? What exactly does God do? Do you ever talk to Him? Does He ever talk to you? Does He really hear everybody's prayers?

Do our souls really live eternally? What is "eternal life" anyway? The only way I can relate to eternal is, missing you is eternal!

Sweetheart, can you see us? Do you hear us? Baby, do you miss us? Is love the same there as it is here?

Will you always be 17? Is there really reincarnation? If there is and you come back here, how will I know? How will I ever see you again? Matthew, you'd just better stay right where you are now until I get there!

Dear God, PLEASE let me be with Matthew!

The journal's funding went away in November and we wrapped up its final issue. I declined the job of editing the small tabloid that replaced it, in effect, throwing away my emotional superstructure of work, and life became a job search, a mortgage and my prayer.

Shortly before Christmas I had my first dream about Matthew since his death. I saw myself standing on one side of a street and Matthew and Michael approaching on the other side. I was overjoyed! As I ran to them I saw that Michael's body was solid, normal, but Matthew's was translucent. I hugged him and said, "Matthew, you're ALIVE!" He said, *"Mother, of course I am!"* I wakened, feeling a mixture of happiness and sadness and a strong sense that I should go back to Washington.

I did that as soon as I could after returning from Florida, where Eric, Betsy, Michael and I spent the holidays with my mother. Through a rapid and unlikely series of coincidences, one being an area-wide blizzard that immobilized most transportation, a friend and I met Fred, the first medium who was "visited" by Matthew. During the next month, through more coincidences, I learned of two other mediums, Olga in Maryland and Laura in New Jersey, and they, just like Fred, asked only my son's name before saying that his spirit left his body before the vehicle crashed and he witnessed it painlessly from above. They all described him— his age, stature, coloring, even his endearing crooked smile— it absolutely was Matthew they were seeing!

According to those three who spoke for him, to whom I offered no more information than "Matthew Ward" because they didn't ask for any, he was very close to all of his family and wanted us to stop grieving for him because it wasn't helping any of us. He was distressed because his father felt guilty and there was no reason for it, and he wanted me to tell that to his father. He had read a book that had helped him prepare for what happened. He wanted us to know he had a full and wonderful life now. Through his translators, he related news about himself as well as specific comments that showed unmistakably he knew about my activities and feelings. And all of the mediums told me that when the time was right, Matthew and I would communicate directly. Missing him still was agonizing, but I was beginning to know what my boy was up to!

Are you wondering if I was deluding myself, stretching generalities and lucky guesses into hazy specifics that let me *imagine* my son's new life? You judge for yourself, but before that, I want to state that this book isn't to recount what I heard *about* Matthew many years ago. It's to share with you what I've heard *from* him during the past few years. The inclusion here of a few messages I received via those mediums has purposefulness as significant as the link they were between my life and Matthew's.

First, skeptics could conclude that I have concocted my lengthy conversations with Matthew, that maybe unusually prolonged grieving finally resolved itself by kicking in an imaginary contact with him that I think is real. The messages from those mediums prove that telepathic communication is not anyone's imagination. Second, those messages reveal the intimate and enduring bonds between us on Earth and the people we love who have left. My personal experiences are profound examples of this.

———————————

When a cousin and I were standing by Matthew's body in the morgue, I was feeling a strange sense of peace that Matthew wasn't there. I did feel sad because I couldn't after all do what I had looked forward to, hold my son in my arms one last time. I just looked at him and didn't feel moved to touch him. I was hearing a dialog. One voice was urging: "Go ahead, hold him! That's why you came here, to hold him one more time. You're his mother—how can you NOT want to hold him!" The other voice argued: "It's different from what you thought it would be. That is his body, but it isn't Matthew. He doesn't need it anymore and it's all right if you don't hold it." I did after all reach out to touch him, and a powerful force pushed my hand away. I left in composure and told the waiting family, "It's all right, that isn't Matthew."

Matthew told Fred about that occurrence in the morgue. He described the room and said he had watched me from his place near the ceiling. He said that his soul energy had pushed my hand away before I touched his cold body. He was surrounding me with loving energy to shield me from the trauma of seeing his body.

When Betsy and I were cleaning Matthew's room and sorting through school papers in his desk, we found a book report he had written. It was good, and it had been graded accordingly, but we doubted if Matthew had written it all himself. He was bright, and he was an accomplished writer, but some unusual wording in one spot just "wasn't Matthew," we agreed, and so we decided that he'd had a helper— probably some girl who was smitten. I kept his notebooks and the book report.

Fred told me that Matthew was disturbed because I doubted that he had done some particular schoolwork. He wanted me to look in a notebook, where I'd find proof that he had done that work himself, and he wanted his sister to know that, too. Fred said that whatever it was that Matthew was referring to, he sounded really indignant that his sister and I didn't give him credit for doing it.

When I returned home I looked through his notebooks and found the first draft of his report on "Sybil." There was the same wording that Betsy and I had questioned. I read his final report, too, and this time I noticed something that both Betsy and I had overlooked before: The short paragraph containing the wording that "wasn't Matthew" was properly punctuated and attributed to the book's author.

Matthew told Fred that I loved classical music, and he was taking piano lessons so he could learn to feel that way about it too. He said that my knowing this would answer one of my "big questions."

I had been wondering why I couldn't hear my favorite symphonies without thinking of Matthew even more intently than usual. I had long felt passionate about that music but couldn't understand why I had started to associate it with Matthew, who hadn't learned to even tolerate it.

A few weeks later Laura told me that Matthew was playing a piano and wanted me to know he was still at it. She added that he needed a lot more practice.

Fred told me Matthew was studying medicine. He referred to it as "armchair medicine" because he had just started and was not yet applying what he was learning. Without my mentioning anything of this to Olga or Laura, both said Matthew was progressing well with his medical studies. A year later, when I met the medium who became my link with Matthew for several years—again, without my offering any information—I received a progress report on his advanced medical and psychology studies and his promotions in his work helping transitioning souls.

After Matthew and I made our connection, he told me about his work in great detail.

When I traveled to New Jersey, where Laura lived, her husband greeted me and hung up the green ski jacket I wore, then told me how to get to the room where she was waiting for me. As we were having tea after the "reading," Laura said Matthew was insisting that she tell me to stop wearing his green jacket and start wearing my new white coat that had just been hanging in the closet, and she asked if that made any sense to me.

I had bought the white wool coat shortly before Matthew died and hadn't had an occasion to wear it during those few weeks before I left so quickly for Panama. Throughout the cold months I'd worn his jacket simply for warmth, and when winter came again, I wore it simply because it was his. (Despite his message, I just couldn't put on the white coat or give up his jacket, which I continued to wear until late spring.)

Those revelations were incomparably uplifting because, even without exact images of Matthew's whereabouts, I felt more connected with him. The most revealing proof of our inseparability, though, was confirmed during my meeting with the first medium. Matthew said that when I was in his room, I saw something in his notebook that showed me he knew his time on Earth would be ending soon. He said I was right in what I thought, that he did know he would not be in this world much longer, and I realized this because his and my souls were breaking through to my consciousness.

Just before his memorial service I was leafing through one of his notebooks that I hadn't seen before. I couldn't absorb anything he had written, but I needed that closeness with him. Suddenly there was the page with large block letters: **I BELONG TO NOBODY.** *I whispered, "Matthew, you knew, didn't you?" and I heard, "Yes, Mother, I knew."*

COMMUNION WITH MATTHEW

During the years between Matthew's death and our first contact, I kept thinking about what all the mediums had said, "when the time is right," he and I would communicate directly. Despite their apparent certainty that this would happen, I couldn't help but doubt it.

Why would I ever be able to do something as "divine," which it seemed to me, as talk with my son in Heaven? I'm not remarkable in any way, not by beliefs or intelligence or training in any areas thought of as New Age thinking and practices. Although I had been told that everyone has the capacity for telepathic communication—it is our birthright, inherent in our souls—I felt innately unprepared, maybe even unworthy of what I still considered a rare gift. I'd never had premonitions, prophetic dreams or a sensation of déjà vu. When the phone rang, I never "knew" who was calling before I answered. Even Matthew's call the night before he died gave me no inkling of anything beyond his words, and so, with good reason, I had no conviction that someday while I was still on Earth we actually would connect.

What I did have was *hope* and *desire* that we would. And I imagined that if we did, occasionally I could ask him myself about his life, and I would receive short answers like his comments to the mediums.

Almost fourteen years passed and I was far away from the dear woman who had been my only link with Matthew from 1982 until 1990, when I moved far from her home in San Diego. After that, until her health failed, I called her occasionally to get updates on him. Finally, I started asking God to give me a neon sign with directions for reaching my son, and maybe that's why our contact came about as it did. One night I was wakened by a lighted ticker tape moving through my mind: *"Mother, this is Matthew. Yes, it really is Matthew."* I thought it must be a creation of my years of wanting contact so much, and I greeted only with pondering what truly was his first message.

In a quiet moment the next day, when my mind was floating somewhere tranquil, I heard the same message. I couldn't help but think, "Am I talking to myself, making believe it's Matthew?" even as I had a sense that something unusual was happening.

Someone suggested that I try automatic writing and explained the simple process. Pen and yellow pad in hand, I concentrated on the letter I was writing to Matthew. I didn't hear anything and no unseen force moved my pen. I tried not to feel discouraged when nothing extraordinary happened the following day, either. My third attempt brought some clearly-expressed thoughts I felt weren't my own. That is, they were coming as if parallel with mine, like a mile of railroad tracks having separate, different ideas at the same time. Simultaneously with my thinking, "This could be Matthew at last, it really could be!" I was hearing, *"Please listen to what I want to tell you."* My excitement prompted me to start writing what I was hearing and not wait for the pen to do anything on its own. Matthew told me he'd been waiting a long time to reach me, that my years of stress had prevented my smooth energy flow, which was essential for our connection, but now we had it.

That was our beginning.

Our conversations quickly became longer and progressively astonishing, and after a few days I switched from writing to a computer. Every morning for about an hour Matthew and I had a "sitting"—that's what I call our con-

versations—when he talked about his life and Heaven.
Once again I could picture my son in his surroundings so
far away from my own!

As jubilant as I was, still I wondered if some phenom-
enon was letting my mind form his part of our discussions
until I considered the several differences between my
thoughts and what he was telling me. The incoming information flows into my head near the top, whereas my mus-
ing seems to be at a lower level. Matthew (and all the other
sources who came later) speaks at a normal conversational
pace. He doesn't hesitate, as if searching for a specific word
or how to most clearly express his meaning. That's unlike
my thinking process, which often is only key words or the
"Yes!" sensation of a whole idea. Also, in contrast to
Matthew's dependable uninterrupted flow, at times I speak
hesitantly as I determine which words will be the most pre-
cise or diplomatic.

Some of Matthew's most often used words I know but
never use, and on occasion his words were entirely new to
me. But the most significant proof that I wasn't somehow
fabricating the transmissions came when information totally
alien even to my imagination, let alone my comprehension,
started coming. Then I knew the source was light years
beyond my head.

I was stunned when I learned that I talk not only with
my Matthew, but also his *cumulative soul.* Now and always
his own unique, inviolate self, Matthew also is an inseparable part of a much greater being who is more spiritually
evolved and knowledgeable than its individual lifetimes. So
that I could understand this shocking revelation, I asked
him for a simple explanation about his relationship as my
son to his cumulative soul, and he told me this:

I was to think of all creation as an ocean, of his cumula-

*tive soul as a cup of ocean water and of his soul as only
Matthew as a drop of water I took from the cup. The drop
was now its own entity, separate from the other drops that,
combined, were the cupful, and from the ocean, where all the
drops originated. Both the single drop and the cupful retained the same elements as the ocean and for a while they
had a life independent of their origin and each other, but
eventually both would return to the ocean. Perhaps the drop
would evaporate into the air, like countless drops before it,
and rise to help form a cloud that would release its vapor
into rain that would fall into the ocean. Perhaps the cup would
spill, letting all of its drops mingle with the sand, where
soon the tide would rush in to cover that part of the shore.
Over and over: the single drop, the cupful of drops, the ocean
that gave them their beginning and would take them back.
Yet never would the individual identity and experiencing of
the drop or the cupful be lost. This timeless, indestructible
interconnectedness acknowledges the uniqueness and value
of each tiny drop (each soul) and each cupful (cumulative
soul) as parts of the ocean (all of creation).*

Matthew said this interconnectedness is true of
everyone's soul, not only when we reach his world, but constantly, continuously, eternally we are inseparable from all
other souls and our Creator. At soul level we do know this;
however, most of us don't consciously know it during Earth
lifetimes.

Because Matthew is the most recent part of his cumulative soul in relation to me, he's the predominant personality in our communion. He refers to his lifetime as my son
as his Matthew *personage.* In the beginning it was difficult
for me to think about two Matthews, my son and the greater
soul that includes my son. But with time, the unnatural
association became completely natural. I call both Mat-

thew, both call me Mother. And rightly so, as it is *only*
Matthew with whom I'm communicating, whether his personage or cumulative soul is speaking.

My perspective of this duality is his gaining such great
knowledge during a long absence that, upon his return, even
to me he sometimes seems a stranger because I missed all
of his incremental growth stages. Other times he is the
young man I remember so well, yet knew only partly, because a mother never can completely know the mind and
heart of her child, even one who has never left home.

In the beginning only the personage was apparent because the topics were personal to Matthew, so that aspect of
his cumulative soul naturally was predominant, and I could
easily imagine my teenaged son talking with his usual enthusiasm. Nevertheless, in our communication just as in
every other facet of his spirit life, he draws upon the multiple lifetime experiences and knowledge that form the total essence of his cumulative soul; and as his information
advanced in complexity, his presentation changed into a
learned, didactic style.

Often even within the same conversation the styles are
seesaw fashion. Matthew told me that my interest and reaction to what I hear are registered as energy vibrations.
When I'm feeling close in spirit to him, my vibration evokes
his personage, and when my interest in the information is
more academic than personal, that vibration calls forth his
cumulative soul.

When the personage is dominant, Matthew's voice is
expressive, and his speech is animated and rambling, sometimes flippant. His exuberance, pet expressions and sense of
humor that I used to enjoy so much still flavor his comments.
Except that Matthew does a lot more talking than I—
he gives long answers to my short questions—we have a

perfectly natural conversation with all the affection and pleasure of any mother and son chatting on Earth.

The voice of the cumulative soul is certain and steady, and the articulate speaking is like a professor presenting a lecture. Whereas Matthew's personage says his bit and then pauses to give me my turn, and without my asking, addresses my mental questioning or reactions to what he's telling me, his cumulative soul continues until the dissertation is complete or my vibration switches.

During the first few sittings with primarily the cumulative soul speaking, I felt more amazement than closeness as I recorded the transmissions. It didn't seem at all like my Matthew, and I felt as if I were back in school taking lecture notes. This bothered me, but I never mentioned it. One morning he (his cumulative soul) said:

I know you have been concerned about your feelings toward me that sometimes are less personal than they used to be. Don't be, Mother. It is an over-layer of feeling that provides the emotional distancing necessary for you to respect my words as coming from a higher source than your 17-year-old Earth son.

I was relieved to hear that, but I wasn't surprised that he knew of my discomfort. I learned almost immediately that he knows many of my thoughts and feelings. Although he has assured me of complete privacy of thought, feeling and action when I wish, when I am open telepathically in either sittings or strong thoughts of him at any moment, there is no place in my mind or heart he cannot touch. This is what enables him to address my thoughts and feelings as he continues talking without any interruptions from me.

I can see Matthew, from images he forms for me, alone or with the souls dearest to him in his spirit home. When his comments make me laugh, I hear and sometimes also see him laughing with me. I feel the warmth of his embrace just as surely as I do the hugs of someone on Earth. In our sittings, there is no distance between us.

Another wonderful surprise about my telepathic connection was that it isn't limited to Matthew. My parents and friends occasionally have joined in our sittings, and I have received messages from people I've never known, requested by their loved ones whom I do know. Matthew has introduced many other souls to me. Some live in his world, others are collective energies whose vastness in power and distance from Earth are, to me, incomprehensible.

Not long after our communion started, Matthew announced that I was to prepare in manuscript form the information I received from him and soon would receive from a number of other sources. That would be an enormous undertaking that I had no time for or interest in, and I ignored him. Later, just as he had said, those other sources did come—by invitation of the Council of Nirvana and with formal presentations especially for publication, I was told. Still, even with those astounding messages and Matthew's frequent pleas, *"Start the book,"* I had no intention of doing that.

Matthew and I were at an impasse of sorts. I was resisting doing what he kept asking me to do, and he was avoiding an issue, too. He never gave me a straight answer about why he had died so young. When he had told me about our family's pre-birth agreement, he'd said that every one of us had agreed to his leaving when he did, but in my subsequent questioning, always he was evasive about *why* we had agreed. His replies were variations of *"Someday you will know and understand."* I stopped prodding him for an explicit answer when he told me that some aspects of the agreement still caused him sadness.

One morning about six months after our sittings began, when Matthew once again was urging me to start work on "the book," it occurred to me to ask if I had some karmic responsibility to do that. After an uncustomary pause, he said:

If you consider that all living is karmic, then yes, that is correct. But far more correct is that preparing this information for a book is your primary mission of this lifetime. Now you can understand why I was so reluctant to explain the reason for my leaving Earth when I did. Without my leaving, you could not have performed your mission. It also was for my own soul growth, but it was mainly to pave the way for this larger service you are performing. Mother, please see the importance of this service in perspective to the world. You see the beauty of Earth, and within your hands lies ability to help in its preservation.

My son had died for a book.

Grief and rage overwhelmed me. It was unthinkable that I had agreed to sacrifice my son for anything! But a book. Just a book. I couldn't see through my tears. Then, the voice was so gentle I wasn't sure I really was hearing it, but when I could see again, I read this, the same message, on my computer screen:

Now let me say that this is not only Matthew but the most gentle and highest Light that is barely moving the keys in its tenderness. I AM that I AM. It is the Way, the Truth, and the Light. It is the Father God of all creation on Earth and this universe giving forth love and shining radiance for this work of full service ahead. So be it. Amen.

Our family's soul level agreement became my source of energy and inspiration as I accepted the commitment I didn't remember making, at some time I couldn't relate to, in some dimension of my soul I don't consciously know. In wonderment and humility, I began the work that in another lifetime, another world, Matthew and I agreed to undertake.

PART II

NIRVANA

FIRST IMPRESSION

S: Matthew, tell me about Heaven.

MATTHEW: Life is meaningful, Mother! There is an ecstasy, a fervor among the people here. We have important work, almost limitless studies, visits to Earth families, glorious music, astounding travel and incomparable beauty. *Much* more goes on here than the blissful life in spirit that is associated with Heaven!

Nirvana is the proper name of this realm. Often it is referred to as a haven, and maybe from that use the word Heaven came. This is a placement mainly for people who have left their Earth bodies and are on their next stage of spiritual evolvement; however, many transient souls live here, too. Despite the great difference between the usual concept of Heaven and the actuality of life here, this *is* the "eternal life" of Earth religions.

ETHERIC BODIES

S: Do you have some kind of body or only an ephemeral essence?

MATTHEW: I definitely have a body, Mother! We have etheric bodies. You might think of Earth bodies as being the tight weave of chintz compared with our bodies being the loose weave of cheesecloth. Each material has its definite shape, weight and thread structure, but the cheesecloth has greatly more flexibility and motion and versatility because it's less dense than the more tightly woven fabric.

We can stand or sit, just as you can, but our bodies also can float in a conscious state as well as in a resting state, like your sleep. Also, we can move within or without our bodies, and we can see each other either way.

Our bodies are less dense than yours because they vibrate at a higher frequency than bodies on Earth. Our vibratory rate is considerably higher than your third density vision can register, which is why most people on Earth can't see us even when we're standing right beside them.

S: Then how can some spirits be seen at séances?

MATTHEW: Dense bodies are created for the visiting spirits whose lighter etheric bodies could not be seen. Those temporary bodies are created from plasma generated by the trance medium and fragments of energy that are amalgamated from volunteers in this realm.

S: That's interesting. Please tell me more about etheric bodies.

MATTHEW: They are perfect in form and function in accordance with the soul's evolution. Souls who had imperfect physical bodies due to genetic deformities or disabling disease or injury are not subjected to those in their etheric bodies. With soul evolvement both men and women become taller and leaner than most Earth humans, and our babies and little children automatically grow into that form. And neither our bodies nor our mental faculties tire, so time away from work or studies isn't necessary for resting, only for our other interests and enjoyment.

We retain features that are as close as we wish to our former appearance. People who feel they were unattractive in their Earth lifetime may request to refine their features, but such changes are not an open option. If the request is in alignment with spiritual development, it is granted, but if it's motivated by ego, it isn't. Enlightenment about full growth into beauty—mental, emotional, physical and spiritual beauty—is offered as a regular study that would be like your self-improvement courses.

When Earth lifetimes have been distinguished by notable achievements, this is evident in our appearance. Our auras are brighter and more distinct in the certain color tone ranges that identify the areas of excelling. Actually, it's less a color variation and more a glowing capacity difference—we radiate our health and spiritual evolvement. It's comparable to your glistening eyes that reflect contentment, enthusiasm, innocence, love—all of the qualities and characteristics associated with godly character and behavior.

S: Matthew, what do you look like now?

MATTHEW: I'll *show* you, Mother. . . . Good! You are clearly receiving the image I'm sending, so you can see I look just like you remember me—tall and slim with the same olive skin, gray eyes and light brown hair. Yes, a little older, as you're thinking, but that would be true if I had been there all along, you know.

S: You are as handsome as ever! Mash, you look just like you would if you had grown older here.

MATTHEW: I just looked older more quickly here, Mother. Our aging is different from yours. Young people here grow much faster than on Earth in body, mind and spirit until they reach maturity in body that would correspond to healthy, robust Earth humans 30 to 35 years in age. At that point they maintain that body and continue to grow only in mind and spirit.

The reverse is true for people who arrive in their advanced years. The older folks grow younger in all respects at that same accelerated pace until they reach that prime year period. I'm referring to . . . .

S: But when I get there, how will I recognize my parents? They'll look younger than I can remember them, and both were short and plump.

MATTHEW: You'll recognize them instantly through the energy attachment, the love bonding—it will be unmistakable, Mother! If they want to appear as you remember them, they could do that, but I can assure you, it wouldn't be necessary because you'll know them immediately.

S: Thank you, and please excuse me for interrupting.

MATTHEW: Your typed question didn't interrupt me, I knew it as soon as you thought it. Your thoughts are the interruptions in my own thinking process, but I realize they're unavoidable.

I was about to clarify that I wasn't speaking of soul growth forward or backward, but only the etheric body and rejuvenated psyche of the newcomer. Once acclimated to this realm, everyone's vibratory rate remains at an optimum status, because at soul level no one is sick or injured or incapacitated by mental or physical debilities.

Souls of all ages are present, of course, since new people arrive continuously and their transition ages range from newborn to past 100 years. Only the very oldest and the very youngest can be absolutely recognized as newcomers. Probably at least half of those who appear to be about 30 to 35 years old and in fine health are long-timers. A long-timer may have been here for only 20 years, however, and often less. Many souls make their transition during that range of prime Earth ages, so after they receive all necessary care and adjust to the realm, those who had sound bodies naturally appear much like the same person they were when they left Earth. Well, maybe a lot healthier and happier!

ENVIRONMENT

S: What does Nirvana look like?

MATTHEW: It's BEAUTIFUL! Imagine a cloudless sky of blue that's almost blinding in its crystalline purity. Periods comparable to the spans of dawn and dusk on Earth are the only change from the brilliance of this blue light, and in those times there is an intense golden haze. Along with green of the same intensity, those are our primary colors.

S: Is there solid ground?

MATTHEW: Yes, but like all other facets of our world, the ground isn't of the same composition as yours. The ground covering, which we call *virna,* is edible, just as grass is for your grazing animals, and it's as plush as an easy chair.

Although our scenery, too, is of a different density than yours, we have incredibly beautiful areas similar to those on Earth. I especially enjoy being at a lake where the water is crystal clear and reflects the overhanging trees. These trees are taller than your redwoods but with more delicate trunks, and they have fragrant rose-colored blossoms. The white sandy soil of the shoreline feels like talcum powder.

S: Thank you for that image, dear. What a heavenly place that is!

MATTHEW: Well, this is *Heaven,* Mother! That lake and our oceans and mountains and forests could be called static, or stable, scenery, because they always are here.

We can create our private surroundings, including weather, to delight us momentarily and we can change them as often as we wish. The seasons change here somewhat like on Earth because enough of us desire those differences. Generally we have what you could call "just another perfect day in paradise" because that's what the majority want and, as a collection of individuals, they create it. For instance, people at an outdoor concert or fiesta don't want a storm to interrupt their enjoyment, so they don't create one. But elsewhere someone who wishes the drama of thunder and lightning can conjure it up wherever he is and it's confined to his presence. Whatever environment anyone wants, he manifests in his immediate surroundings without affecting anyone outside of that encapsulated zone.

S: Matthew, that's just mind-boggling, making whatever weather and scenery you want!

MATTHEW: It is an advantage, for sure, but it isn't the limit of our manifesting ability. *Whatever* can be envisioned clearly and desired intently can be manifested here, where the sensory and creative capacities of the soul are more optimally developed and used than on Earth.

NOURISHMENT

S: Is your food anything like ours?

MATTHEW: Our bodies don't need dense nourishment, and the longer people are here, the less desire they have for solid food. However, since eating is such an enjoyable pastime on Earth, when most souls arrive they still want the familiarity of eating rituals and comfort, and so we have numerous types of delicious food to accommodate them. A lot of us enjoy eating picnic style.

Some of our food is like your fruit, ready to eat right off the tree or bush. Other foods, more like your vegetables, usually are cooked and flavors are added. But no animals are turned into dinner!

I haven't been eating for quite some time because it no longer appeals to me. I do like liquids, though. We have many types of delicious and invigorating drinks. Some resemble light fruit juices with an effervescence that actually is light sparkles mixed with the liquid. Other, denser liquids taste like your vegetable soup with various seasonings.

Water here is purer than any on Earth and it also has captured light bubbles. And there is liquid in the air, like mist, which is both refreshing and nourishing for our bodies just in the contact.

S: Would that contact be equivalent to our bathing?

MATTHEW: No. Bathing here has nothing to do with dirty bodies—we simply don't "get dirty"—it is a refreshing experience involving a mental outlook, not soap and water. It's the same for our animals. Wouldn't that be wonderful for you, with your six dogs!

S: For me, that really would be Heaven on Earth!

HEAVEN ON EARTH

MATTHEW: Mother, let me be very serious for a moment. Yes, for you that would indeed be "Heaven on Earth" because that is how you feel about it. There is no "Heaven" as a placement, nor a "hell" as such. What people on Earth refer to as Heaven and hell actually are their approaches to situations *wherever* they are, and what each individual manifests as the circumstances of his life.

Every single soul there creates his surroundings, and they are different from even the same "set of props" as they appear to those who are sharing that life in any close capacity. It is a matter of individual *perception* that creates each individual world, and one can *choose* how he wishes to perceive all aspects of his life. It is just as easy to create the glories you attribute to Heaven as it is to create the horrors you associate with hell, and both conditions are being created right there!

You have heard people say that someone "is creating his own hell," or "Heaven and hell are right here on Earth." YES! And neither as perceived there is in this spirit realm.

ORIGIN

S: Well, if our concepts of Heaven and hell are so differ-
ent from their actuality, what is the purpose of Nirvana?

MATTHEW: Its original purpose was different from
its current one, which is primarily a residential and learning placement. In this context, it is the home of souls between incarnations on Earth, but it serves other very
important purposes, too.

When life forms with intelligence and conscience were
first created, there was no need for a realm like this. Aging as we know it didn't exist at that stage of antiquity, so
physical death from "old age" was not a consideration. It
was the cosmic battling that started between the dark and
the light forces that created the need for Nirvana and other
similar placements. The light beings realized that safe
havens were needed for their wounded or exhausted souls
who would be easy prey for the dark forces, and they created many realms like this one to protect and preserve
their frail, recovering kindred spirits.

I should mention that *light* equates with wisdom, love
and the power of love, and *dark* is the absence of all that. In
another sense, it could be considered the opposing sides,
respectively, of positive and negative use of energy, the life
force of all that has ever been created. The two opposing
forces have been waging war ever since the first darkly-
inclined beings used their free will to create and proliferate
negativity in our universe.

S: Matthew, I'm not sure I heard you correctly. Did
you say there's more than one Nirvana and that those

places were created by powers other than God?

MATTHEW: As far as I know, there's only one placement named Nirvana, but there are many havens for the
same purpose. This one is primarily for transitioning souls
from Earth, and other worlds have their own discarnate
realms for their inhabitants. In all cases, I am referring to
transition from an *immediate* past physical life to discarnate
life. Many souls here now originated in deep antiquity and
have spent many lifetimes in places other than Earth, even
in other galaxies.

Mother, intelligent human life did not originate on
Earth. It was introduced there by physical relocation of
humans from other planetary systems and their populat-
ing programs at a crucial point in the evolution of Earth
human root stock. So, in the sense of our ancestry, ALL of
us are extraterrestrial to Earth even during our lifetimes
on the planet!

As for the creation of all these haven realms, the creating powers certainly were *of* God. Creator's, or God's, gift
of free will includes its inseparable aspect of manifesting
capability *in conjunction with Him.* An individual's creating ability never is separate from God's. *Souls never are
separate from God!*

Nirvana and similar realms are manifestations of the
angels and their highest-being descendants, whom they also
had co-created with God. So you see, it was from that lower
level of decision-making and co-creative ability that the restorative, protected placements such as Nirvana came into
being.

S: What do you mean, Nirvana is a "manifestation"?

MATTHEW: Manifestation, or creation, if you will, is

both the process and the product of a joint creating effort between Creator or God and any soul using universal elements as building materials. In the process, first comes the idea, or the vision, then the intense desire to put that idea into substance, then the rest of the effort required to do so. That process of manifestation results in the product, *a* manifestation. Just as this realm is a manifestation, so is Earth. So are *you! Everything* in the universe from a galaxy to an acorn to a jet plane is a manifestation. The creating capability of all beings, whether living in body or in spirit, originates within Creator. Therefore there is no separation between Creator, or God, and any co-creator, just as there is no separation between God, or Creator, and everything that has ever been created.

Mother, I know I've been going back and forth between "God" and "Creator" as if they're one and the same. They aren't. I've only confused you by trying to explain things within your capacity to relate, and you know of only that one "supreme being," whom you call God. But the ultimate power of the cosmos—the omnipotent, omniscient essence, the Totality, I AM, or any of the other designations you have for God—actually is Creator.

At the time of the "Big Bang," a reference sometimes given to that first dividing of Creator, the highest realm of angels—the archangels—was created. That's where the Christed energy resides. That division was not a diminishing of Creator's essence, but a proportionate sharing of powers even as the whole remained. The archangels were not of substance, only of pure love expressed as light.

Eons later, in conjunction with Creator, the archangels created the next level of angels, who also were only light and also shared proportionately Creator's powers. In the third step of creation, the angelics in conjunction with Creator made life form potentials, meaning that manifestations now could be discarnate or of substance. They created the universes—which combined are the cosmos—with all of their celestial bodies and the gods who went forth to rule and co-create all life within the universes. One of those gods became ruler of our universe, and many Earth religions call him God. God has proportionately all the powers of Creator, and in this universe, He rules with those qualities you rightfully attribute to Him. And even though He is referred to as "Father" and with masculine pronouns, God is total love and light, which has no gender.

S: Matthew, I know you're trying to explain this as simply as you can, but it's going to take a few readings before I can comprehend it enough just to ask sensible questions.

MATTHEW: I understand that, Mother. At one time the people of Earth knew all about their Creator-God connection and manifestation and life in this realm. There was continuous passage back and forth then between here and there, and constant telepathic connection. All of that has been forgotten there—the knowledge has been suppressed by the dark forces. They can't change the truth, they can only try to keep it hidden from you. But just as your physics has mathematically proven the time and space continuum, it could prove our inseparable connection within the same universal laws.

RESIDENTS

S: How many souls live in Nirvana?

MATTHEW: Between 10 and 12 billion. We come and go continuously, so the population fluctuates. You're having a hard time with that number, Mother. Why?

S: It seems like a lot of souls between Earth lifetimes.

MATTHEW: I need to clarify our population, which is considerably more varied than I've explained. Although this realm is primarily for people transitioning from Earth lifetimes, who could be called "regular" residents, many others live here, too, and I'll tell you about all of them.

Although most of our regular residents are preparing for their next lifetime on Earth, depending upon the stage of their soul growth, some are preparing for incarnate or discarnate life elsewhere, even outside our galaxy, or they may choose to experience as free spirits. Probably 20 years is average for a "long-timer," but I'm not really comfortable giving that figure because many variables influence the length of residency. Some souls feel great sensitivity in all aspects, an ability acquired only in higher density vibrations, and they don't stay very long. Some are so highly evolved that they practically whisk through to their next growth placement.

Others of this spiritual evolvement status may choose to remain here quite a while. They have earned this as a reward for honored service, and they stay for a long time by your calculations. Some of these souls are very high in our hierarchy. Other long-timers are here for intensive healing from a number of difficult lifetimes. They stay in an environment of tranquility as long as they need to recuperate before choosing their next level of spiritual growth experiencing. All those souls constitute what I referred to as our "regular" population.

Another large part is transient. Some are free spirits, who come and go as their growth needs require.

S: Matthew, excuse me, please. Remember, here free spirits are folks who seem to go blithely through life doing their own thing out of the "mainstream." Is it the same there?

MATTHEW: Oh, no, Mother. Free spirit can mean only that no body, not even the etheric body, is necessary for residence of the soul. But in a larger sense it refers to the mental attitude or psychic approach to communion with God and the knowledgeable accomplishing of the pre-birth chosen mission. Either or both of these conditions constitute a free spirit lifetime. It's a different sort of learning process and is as necessary as any other lesson due to karmic cause and effect.

S: I see. Thank you.

MATTHEW: You're welcome! Now then, others of our transients are teachers in specialty fields or students who come for selected education, and they leave when they have accomplished their purpose. Visitors come from other discarnate realms to further their spiritual growth and stay as long as their specific interests last. And there are many short-term vacationers, some from suprahuman civilizations. Nirvana is much more beautiful than many other discarnate realms and, just like resorts on Earth, it attracts "tourists."

There is still another kind of resident here, souls who have taken on new bodies on Earth, but they reside here as well as there. Mother, this isn't "weird" at all, and there is good reason for these "dual" lives. When one is motivated toward studies, learning can be achieved far more rapidly here than on Earth. We have almost limitless superb resources and master teachers, and the entire environment is conducive to spiritual growth. What better place to gain knowledge and spiritual enlightenment with which to endow the new personage?

S: Well, OK. Does that dual life change the two people, like creating "multiple personalities"?

MATTHEW: It doesn't change them at all in the sense of creating a "multiple personality" condition in either. That comes from traumas that the human psyche handles by allowing intolerable experiences to be ascribed to personalities it develops and hides from the "primary personality," who could no longer accept the reality of those experiences.

In the case of "dual" lives, only at *cumulative* soul level is the reincarnated soul both living here and also as the "new" personage on Earth. The cumulative soul encompasses both the "new" and the "old" personages as well as all its other incarnate and discarnate lifetimes. The soul of each of these dual-life personages, like every other soul, is a unique, inviolate being.

This dual life does affect the personage in this realm whose soul has re-embodied, but the change is no different from that in anyone, anywhere, who is growing rapidly in knowledge through studying and in wisdom through experiencing. This growth is assimilated by the cumulative soul and thus it also becomes the "inheritance" of the new personage on Earth.

S: Do the people here who are living dual lives know it?

MATTHEW: Only rarely. Earth's density precludes much of the basic wisdom and knowledge that is usual here. Because of some people's higher soul evolvement, however, closeness between their Earth body and their etheric body easily permits transmuting their energy from the physical plane to the spiritual plane and there is some awareness of the "duality."

I know this will surprise you, Mother—Grandpa is one of the "dual-lifers." He embodied about five years ago as the infant son of a family with financial means and superior intelligence. Grandpa had a fine mind, but as you know, his family's circumstances prevented his being formally educated beyond the eighth grade. What you may not know is that lifelong, that was a source of disappointment and frustration to him.

However, that was part of his pre-birth agreement, and in the new life he has chosen—I should say, his cumulative soul has chosen—to get the education denied in his lifetime as your father. His new family's history indicates that the little boy will be highly educated in professional avenues, most likely law or medicine. To better prepare his cumulative soul's new personage, Grandpa is studying those disciplines here during the boy's sleeping hours to give impetus to the successful application of both advanced studies and innate abilities.

REUNIONS

S: Matthew, I don't know how I feel about my father's new life. I know I should be glad for him because of all the advantages he didn't have before, but when would I ever see him again? You've told me I'd recognize him when I arrive, but surely he can't stay there indefinitely since he has a whole new life on Earth. How can there be any family reunions when the first one who dies already has reincarnated before the others get there?

MATTHEW: Reunions are of the *souls,* Mother. The soul who has embodied on Earth is not bound by the same third density limitations as the physical body and psyche, so it is free to travel wherever it wishes during the sleep or deep meditative states of the person. When there is closeness of souls, their love energy bonding alerts the others—including all those who have embodied again—to the imminent transition of any one. That's why they can be on hand to greet him or her. Often one or more of them may be seen by that person prior to the physical death and understand in a blissful way that very soon he will be going with them.

As for subsequent reunions, always it is possible that they can meet in this realm, and most visits do take place here. However, the souls may meet anyplace in the universe where their energy frequency enables them to go. The soul that has reincarnated has total freedom for travel, and the energy bonding of that soul with any others anywhere will allow reunions wherever all parties wish within their energy limitations.

Mother, here's a perfect example of how easily these visits of beloved souls in various lifetimes can happen—and this also may surprise you—you have visited this realm many times in your sleep state. You seldom consciously remember being here with me or our visits with Grandpa and more recently, Grandma, too. Sometimes you attribute your actual remembering to dreams, which is usual with all people on Earth. Sometimes you think of us and don't realize that it's an actual memory of an actual recent visit with us that's triggering your thought. That, too, is usual with all people there.

S: How I wish I could remember my visits! Is it only the subconscious part of me that goes?

MATTHEW: No, Mother. What comes is your *soul,* the composite of all lifetimes, all experiences, all cellular memory. It is that totally enlightened soul that in this incarnation is YOU who comes. Your visits are no different from those of the embodied souls who gather here to greet a beloved person making transition.

When you're here we communicate without any barriers to comprehension. You have even commented on this, but you don't remember that along with all the rest that is locked out of your consciousness. That forgetfulness is true of almost everyone there, but some who are more advanced in spiritual clarity can remember their visits here to some degree.

S: You're right, my visits are a surprise, my second big one today. Thank you for both, dear! I feel much better now about my father.

MATTHEW: I know, and I apologize, Mother. I felt your distress as soon as you did yourself, and I should

have addressed it immediately. Thank you for this opportunity to expand my awareness of my need for more sensitivity.

*S: Surely it's rare that I could contribute anything to
you, Matthew!*

MATTHEW: On the contrary! We are forever adding to
our awareness with the help of our Earth contacts.

*S: I would never have thought that. About family re-
unions, what if a couple didn't have a good marriage here
and really wouldn't want to be together there. Is there some
way of satisfying both of them?*

MATTHEW: Family members are not automatically
reunited. When there is a reunion, it can only be joyous.
People who never had major dissensions or family conflicts
can meet lovingly on any basis they choose. There are no
restrictions about families being together and interacting
within the high energy of positive characteristics and intentions.

But remember, Mother, when you come to this realm
you won't be only the self you are in this moment, you'll be
the composite of all your lifetimes. You will recognize people
who were significant in your other lifetimes, not only this
one, and you will have love and admiration for them, too.
This is true for all souls, of course, which is one reason
family units don't have to remain as they were during
Earth lifetimes. The marital commission of Earth holds
no sway in this realm. Only love can bind two souls here.
When a soul's love energy is stronger with another soul
than with the former spouse, the joining of the two stronger energies takes precedence.

Nothing may prevent desired unions here. Simply, no

one is around who would object. Those who might object would do so on the basis of negative characteristics, and that energy registration automatically would have placed them in another area of the realm. Understanding that each soul's assignment is designed for growth to overcome negative traits, all souls voluntarily accept their appropriate placements. And there is no room in this part of the realm for the negative feelings and actions that people experience with each other on Earth, family members or not.

S: So there are compartments or categories of life there and they're not the same for everyone?

MATTHEW: Nirvana is a multilayered realm with light placement areas at one extreme and dark at the other. The layer where I'm living is high in the light, and all that I've described to you that's goodness and beauty and growth characterizes this layer's offerings to its residents. People with inclinations toward fear, vengeance, hatred, cruelty, greed and other intense negative emotions can't live in this part of the realm because their density and low frequency can't penetrate this light. By the laws of the universe they cannot enter or survive here. *And that is by their choice!* It goes back to free will. All souls there have free will to live according to their conscience, or lack thereof. Their assignment to the various energetically separated layers of this world is based upon all of their free will choices during their physical lives.

S: Yes, I see. What happens when someone with that negativity nevertheless had been loved on Earth by someone in your part of the realm?

MATTHEW: There will be agreeable separation of the individuals on those incompatible energy levels. For example, two individuals may have cared very much for each other in their incarnation as brothers, but one strayed into negative activities and the other did not. The two can meet and enjoy together whatever activities are on the frequency or density level permitted. Harmony and balance are the key to the energy registrations, and always on that basis of compatibility they can meet. In areas of their dissimilar Earth lifetime inclinations, they cannot meet. Each goes his own way for the next step in his necessary learning. If the negatively-prone brother grows sufficiently in spirituality to live full time in the same layer of the realm as his brother, then the two can be together whenever they want.

S: I see. If a woman remarried after her husband's death and she loved both men, how is that handled when all three are there?

MATTHEW: There are a number of satisfying possibilities. When there are feelings of enlightenment, respect and love among the three, they may choose to live together. There will be no negative feelings if any of them later chooses another soul for companionship in accordance with soul evolvement. Each will be meeting beloved souls from other lifetimes, too, and the woman and the two men may elect singly or all together to live within a reunited soul cluster. Or, even with great affection for each other, they may prefer to live separately and meet on the basis of mutual enjoyment of other souls or shared activities or educational pursuits. Loving, respectful relationships are without complications in whatever configuration is most gratifying to the souls and beneficial to their spiritual growth.

RELATIONSHIPS

S: Is there dating among the young people or any romantic attachment that can lead to an exclusive partnership?

MATTHEW: There's nothing like Earth teenagers' flirtations or infatuations. Souls who come here as infants or little children may grow into young adults who are attracted only to one special person, but their feelings and relationships are quite different from those of a young couple on Earth. Romance there implies sexual desire, which has no part in our attraction to someone. Our bodies are not designed for the same sexual functions as yours because there is no reproduction here, therefore sexual activity doesn't exist either.

But there are many specific two-party unions. In addition to those souls who grew to young adulthood here and become partners, adults who arrive often recognize one another from past incarnations and choose to spend their time together. There is no marriage as you think of it, though, with grand ceremonies and legal documents. Always unions are with the understanding that when one partner decides upon the next incarnate lifetime, the other will not interfere. We know that soul growth is the purpose of all chosen experiencing. It is on the soul level that two people are attracted in the first place, and that same energy bonding will continue in their subsequent lifetimes. That allows these relationships to be fulfilling and without sorrow at the eventual separation for further experiencing.

Nothing here detracts from the happiness felt by any

couple who choose to be together exclusively. They have freedom entirely within the laws of the universe. There is a commitment in their love energy that is respected by all as a sacred trust, so in that sense, you could say it is a marriage even more so than there, where often only a legal formality maintains the marital status.

S: What is the feeling there about divorce here?

MATTHEW: An official divorce of a married couple on Earth is a matter only of acceptance or rejection there. Dissolution of any partnership on Earth is recognized here only in terms of individuals fulfilling or not fulfilling the provisions of their pre-birth agreements. Agreements take into consideration that mates may wish or even need to separate to achieve their souls' chosen experiencing.

S: Can homosexual partners here continue their unions in Nirvana if they want to?

MATTHEW: Yes. Mother, homosexuality is not understood on Earth, and this is a good context in which to explain it. Homosexuality is an evolutionary stage of the spirit even more than an aspect of the physical makeup, and it is not to be condemned or honored any more than any other physical or spiritual stage of development.

Remember, we are dealing with *cumulative* souls here, not single personages. Within each cumulative soul are perhaps as many as thousands of lifetimes of experiencing as male, female and androgynous beings in both incarnate and discarnate bodies. However, it is the *immediate* past life that most emphatically affects the beginning growth state here. If that Earth lifetime was homosexual in orientation, it will enter here the same way. Since our bodies aren't designed for sexual activity, only the mental aspect of the orientation accompanies the arriving soul.

The immediate past Earth lifetime has another impact upon this issue. The people there who most vehemently denounce homosexuality are those whose souls experienced an immediate past lifetime as a personage with that orientation.

S: Matthew, that doesn't make sense to me. I'd think understanding and acceptance would be much more likely.

MATTHEW: It's a complex and confusing psychic situation, Mother. The energy of the personages is still fractured from their immediate previous life experiences. At the extreme, homosexuals have been physically tortured and even killed, and at the least they have been maligned, often even by their families, to such extent that their psyches were severely damaged. Maybe they lived with the pain of denial or shame or the guilt of deception. Whatever their experience, their energy has not healed enough for them to see the very same sorts of traumatic situations they themselves experienced and thus feel empathy. Rather, they see revenge opportunities.

The cycle of experiencing happens so quickly that the pain of memories most recently known, but hidden from consciousness, is with them too closely for the healing that will come in subsequent lifetimes. The lingering pain in the suppressed memories of those souls who in this lifetime chose heterosexual nature causes their extremely antagonistic attitudes toward homosexuals. Those painful feelings will not surface in the form of memories of their homosexual lifetime experiences, but in *attitudes to stifle the memories.*

This is the universal like-attracts-like principle. When the feelings resulting from harsh or unjust treatment in any situation are recent and intense, similar feelings are attracted to that soul. Suppressed memories subconsciously know the source and recall it, thus attracting "like." However, the current lifetime psyche cannot consciously know that the attraction is of *shared* feelings, and the painful sensations of the suppressed memories take over.

Moving forward from that point in the psychic labyrinth comes in the process of lifeprint review, identification of karmic lessons still to be learned, choosing the next lifetime, and progress in spiritual awareness.

S: Do people who were homosexual in their immediate past lifetime always go through what you described, which would seem just to perpetuate things, or is there some leveling out point where all of us will accept each other just as we are?

MATTHEW: The "leveling out" most assuredly is part of the divine plan, because feelings of prejudice and hatred and the infliction of emotional and physical cruelty are impediments to spiritual growth. However, even with the acceleration of light being beamed at your planet to dispel the negativity abounding in humankind, please do not expect this change to be completed within the next generation.

S: Is homosexuality more prevalent now than previously in Earth history?

MATTHEW: No, but there are more people now than previously in your recorded history, so the same percentage creates the greater numbers. Throughout your recorded history well known and highly respected masters in one field or another have been homosexual, and many produced their brilliant and inspiring creations because of their tormented minds regarding this aspect of their nature. You could say that without this element of their personage, they may not have been driven to create in the magnitude and splendor they did.

S: Why is homosexuality a necessary experience?

MATTHEW: How better to learn balance in the two extremes of male and female sexual energy than on an integrated basis? The ideal is androgyny, which has nothing whatsoever to do with human sexual nature, but rather with the two opposites of human sexual *energy* attributes. Androgynous souls are far more spiritually advanced because of the male and female sexual energy balance they have achieved.

Just as male energy is not the province of only male humans, female energy is not confined to female humans. Male energy is harsh, often productive by ruthless means, always needing to prove a point or achieve success in a venture. Female energy is gentle, yet with greater, quiet strength as its foundation. Interconnectedness, which is the ultimate in conscious achievement, is female energy.

In relationships wherein one partner has only male energy traits and the other has only female energy traits, the female energy partner cannot withstand the imbalance lifelong or the life will not be long. In my awareness of such relationships, those which remained in that imbalance ended in early transition of the female energy soul. The survivor often has no frame of reference of his or her involvement in the partner's death. You say "That person— or 'you'—will be the death of me." Like many other common expressions you use, that can be an accurate statement, but few understand the truth of their words. No blame is attributed here to either partner in such a relationship, as in many instances this is no more than karma being fulfilled according to pre-birth agreements. The dissolution of those partnerships by divorce also may be in accordance with the chosen lessons of their agreements.

Any balance within a lifetime is desirable. However, since sexual energy is one of the most essential aspects of the human psyche, the balance of male and female energies is probably the most desirable. In this realm there is that blending of male and female energies insofar as tendencies, sensibilities and sensitivities. That ideal state of balanced reality once existed on Earth, but it was corrupted.

Behaviors stemming from the perversion of the sexual energy stream have proliferated negativity on Earth in such proportions as to be almost unimaginable. By *no* means is sexual energy confined to what you commonly call "wanting sex" or "having sex." Although extending beyond the original intent of the sex drive, which was procreation, a satisfying sexual relationship brings harmony into the lives of loving mates, and I definitely am NOT speaking against a mutually pleasurable, beneficial sexual union. Furthermore, it is possible to transmute sexual energy into other productive avenues, and many who have lost or never had loving mates, do so. But I am not addressing the positive use of this energy, only the rampant negativity created by perversion of the entire sexual energy stream.

This has been the root cause of all that you think of as evil attributes in human nature. There is no crime by your civil, religious or philosophical standards that is not committed from a root cause of sexual energy perversion. As an example, Satanic worship involving the torture and sacrifice of human and animal lives and brutal sexual activities prevails on a scale that would beg disbelief, but is real. This is cloaked under the guise of "religion," and your government officially recognizes it as such! You do not connect either those ungodly practices or their religion status with the perverted use of sexual energy that it actually is.

It shouldn't surprise you that often murder is sexual energy directed into gross deviance, or that rape and incest are other examples. Promiscuous sexual encounters or obsession with either having sex or rigidly refraining from natural urges are more benign, but still destructive to the psyche.

The dark forces are behind all these behaviors resulting from perverted sexual energy. It is not uncommon for the most corrupted activities to lead to the basest of dense energy, and no other aspect of human nature has been so pivotal in alienating a person from God. At soul level there is inseparability, but in physical life, the more corrupt and deviant the sexual energy, the more the people engaging in those activities are distancing themselves from God. Sadly for you and Earth, these free will choices are rampant in your civilization and far from the chosen missions in most of the souls' pre-birth agreements.

Mother, however viewed by many on Earth, a loving homosexual partnership is NOT a perversion of sexual energy, and that brings us back to your question about homosexual unions in this realm. Since there is no condemnation here of people's former sexual orientation, clearly there is no judgment regarding which souls are attracted to each other as mates. Experiencing here on every level is designed for the souls' spiritual evolvement, and that includes all unions. Whether heterosexual or homosexual in nature, the soul level energy and bonding commitment of all couples is totally respected.

DIVINE LOVE, CHILDREN

S: Matthew, is anyone there special to you in a loving way?

MATTHEW: Yes, Mother, there is someone most special to me. I haven't told you before because I don't know how to explain how precious a soul Ithaca is not only to me, but to all who know her. Perhaps the best way to describe the delicacy of her effect upon me and others is by asking you to recall the first moment you held me. Do you remember the perfect purity of your feelings about me, your sense of belonging *with* me but not possessing me or in any way wishing to control me even as your newborn?

S: Matthew, dear, I could never forget that unique feeling, but how do you know about it?

MATTHEW: It's in your lifeprint, a most light-filled event. Think of your feelings then, Mother, and you will know the oneness many of us feel with Ithaca. She is our oversoul entity, and our attachment is on such a rarefied plane that there should be a different level of words to describe this sublime sensation of love. The word "love" has been so ill-used on Earth that it is sadly diluted from its true meaning, but you don't have another word that is any more accurate or encompassing.

Ithaca represents a height in attainment of spiritual beauty that is inspiring to all who know her. She is not my girl friend or lady friend, she is my great love in all purity of admiration and unconditional caring. There is no expectation of a relationship in full union status, but there is a special tenderness between her and me that we both cherish.

The sensations of love here and on Earth are vastly different. There are none of the peaks and valleys of "falling in love" or "being jilted" and none of the sexual chemistry of Earth couples. What we experience that could be compared with your loving sexual unions is a spiritual and etheric bonding with total fusion of energies and shared knowledge of selves. Never is this on the random or promiscuous basis common on Earth. Our unions are sacred experiences, with a spiritual growth unique to this realm. Earth humans' third density sensory mechanisms simply are not capable of this sensation or comprehending it.

A huge group of souls, thousands, can experience the same intensity of bonding. This could be compared to your healing services where many people attend and all lend energy to the event. The level of energy bonding is the same for a young couple whose love is pure and focused. Because the same feelings can be shared by two or two thousand, you can see the major difference between love in this realm and love on Earth!

S: You're right, Matthew, that kind of love is beyond our comprehension. Tell me more about Ithaca, please.

MATTHEW: She is a free spirit in this realm, but she does have an etheric body, so only her closeness with God and total awareness of her soul's chosen mission apply. She is needed and respected throughout the realm for instruction and the healing of minds that were horribly befuddled prior to transition of the soul. Her energy is gentle, almost musical, and this type of healing energy is the most effective for those imbalanced psyches.

Ithaca was a teenager when she arrived here from her last Earth incarnation, during the Incan reign in Peru.

She died as a sacrificial virgin and hasn't wanted to return to a physical life since then. She has evolved at a considerably higher rate than many others who also have chosen to be free spirits.

S: Is this Ithaca I'm seeing?

MATTHEW: Yes, and your vision of her in formal oriental dress is correct, although you are registering disbelief because you were *imagining* her differently. But she is indeed as you see—dainty body, with black hair neatly styled close to her head and slightly almond-shaped eyes. She didn't come here with those features or form, she chose them, and due to her worthy service she was granted that softening evolution into her present appearance.

S: She's lovely! I can actually feel her lilting energy! I'm so happy she is part of your life, Matthew.

MATTHEW: So am I, but Mother, please remember what I told you about her importance to many, many others in this realm who also feel great love for her. Beings like Ithaca are part of the overall magnificence this realm offers.

S: I understand, dear. Why did her image just leave?

MATTHEW: Because your concentration on her diminished and allowed an energy shift.

S: Maybe because I just thought of something else, sort of related. Who do the babies there live with?

MATTHEW: When babies and little children come here before their parents, they are tended by surrogate mothers and fathers and androgynous souls with special aptitudes for nurturing. They live with the children in large cheerful and harmonious homes and give them such abundant love and caring that rarely is it seen on Earth.

Our children are constantly surrounded with love and guidance and playtime and teaching. There are no disputes over their care or instruction as it is by guidance of the Council, and the caretakers acknowledge the wisdom of those guidelines. Just like the adults, all the children here have perfect bodies and health.

S: Can children be adopted if their Earth parents aren't there?

MATTHEW: Yes, after they are old enough to choose a family for themselves. There's no need here for two parents to give a child a well-balanced male and female role image and total family security, so there are single parents, too. If it's considered prudent for the child's development, he or she may spend as much time with potential adoptive parent or parents as all wish.

All children are given highest honor and nurturing, and they provide the family life that is so important to the growth of all souls here. Even though no babies are born in this realm, family love here is one of the most brilliant and sacred manifestations of love in action, not only in sensation.

Mother, I know the questions stirring in your head. Yes, I still have a great enjoyment of little children and, yes, there is a child of special importance to me. You are seeing a smiling little girl with dark curls and big dark eyes. This is Esmeralda. She came here about a year ago, when she was only 18 months old. She has grown to about Earth age four in stature and about age six intelligence level.

S: She's beautiful! Matthew, thank you for letting me see Esmeralda and you together.

MATTHEW: You're welcome, Mother, from both of us.

Esmeralda is from a Mexican family and left many broken hearts when she made her decision to leave after a severe illness left her deaf and blind. That was a case of unplanned destiny—that is, it wasn't within the pre-birth agreement. At soul level she decided not to endure the difficulties she would encounter and not to impose the hardships on her financially poor family if she remained.

So we have Esmeralda here, and she is a joy to many of us. She is most especially dear to me. I am her godfather, in Earth terms. I don't consider her mine, but in affection and loyalty, you could say we belong to each other in love. She spends a lot of time with me, but she needs more personal attention than I can give her, so it's better for her to usually live with other children in that nurturing atmosphere I described.

Ithaca and I often take her to a park by our favorite lake and all of us enjoy those outings. We have picnics and swim and play children's games. If other people are in the same area and we would like company, we join them if they invite us, or vice versa. In this respect, you could say we are like any happy family on Earth having a wonderful time.

Already Esmeralda sings beautifully, and it's anticipated that she will have a professional voice when she's older. Here, singing isn't considered just a talent, but a gift to be shared. For now, I want only to cherish her and not know more about her "future" than if I were her father on Earth. I know you can understand that, Mother. And I know you appreciate my sharing her with you, like a heavenly little granddaughter.

ANIMALS

S: Matthew, are Freckles and Snoopy and Charley there?

MATTHEW: All of them are here, and also your dogs I never knew because they came to you after I left. Of those, Tango is the one most often with me, probably because of the unique bonding between him and you and you and me, but he spends most of his time with Esmeralda.

S: I'm so glad he's there with you and her! After all these years, we still miss that little guy. Are all Earth animals there?

MATTHEW: Most of them, but not all. It's not that those who aren't here are unworthy, but only that the nature of some wild animals is not adaptable out of their native environment, and we don't have zoos or cages. The whole family of large cats, for instance, do have temperaments that are malleable for living peaceably when they're out of the food chain environment of Earth, so they all are here, and of course your pet cats are, too.

S: Why can't all of our fierce animals be adapted to live there?

MATTHEW: Some animals' DNA just can't be adapted to a gentler temperament. The rhinoceros, for example. Its brain doesn't allow for the transmutation of that fierce energy into something benign, so it is one that cannot enter or survive in our refined density. It was more practical to transmute the energy of all the non-adaptable animals into positive life forms than to make the effort to turn them into household pets. But we do have masterfully realistic holographic forms of those animals for teaching purposes and the delight of our children and adults, too.

At the opposite end of the animal life scale are our beloved dolphins and whales, the most intelligent and spiritually evolved of all. Here their bodies are far less bulky than on Earth, but they still are adapted to marine life and their personality is unchanged. On Earth the huge form of the whales is required for holding the light frequency in their environment and for communication, but that isn't necessary here as ideal circumstances have been created for them. Not all of their cumulative Earth energy is in this realm, only enough to create the human-whale energy bonding.

It's somewhat the same situation with your fish. The basic energy of overall fish life there is created here in only two dozen or so species with brilliant colors and extraordinary features and shapes, but we do have all of the familiar and exotic birds of Earth. All of your farm animals are here, of course, and elephants, camels—all the herbivores you have in zoos except the rhino. We have snakes, but those that are poisonous there aren't venomous here. You may not be overjoyed about the snakes, Mother, but you'll be glad to know that we have butterflies and no nuisance insects.

S: Great—no more fleas or flies! Matthew, do animals there remember the people and animals in their Earth lifetimes?

MATTHEW: Beloved pets do indeed "remember" their Earth human and animal families. However, it is by love energy bonding and not by active memories such as you have, with images and recall of voices. Their bonds don't need memories to keep them intact.

S: So animals really do feel love!

MATTHEW: Absolutely, Mother! When animals receive loving treatment, not only do they feel the love given them, they feel love in return. It is the energy principle of "like attracts like," but it is more than that. Animals have an innate capacity to feel many emotions that too few people attribute to them. The higher the level of intelligence, the wider range of possible emotions the animals may feel. Dogs can experience almost all the emotions humans do except those that can be called "sophisticated," like deceit, doubt, encouragement—the types of sensations that you learn through indoctrination and experience.

S: I've always felt that animals had feelings like ours, but I'm glad for this confirmation. When animals that lived together on Earth reach your realm, are they drawn together by love bonds, too?

MATTHEW: Animal energy is attracted to other animal energy because the same wavelength is involved. When love bonds are present—and often they are—a special frequency on the wavelength reaches the animals and, just as with humans, they are reunited by choice via the love bonding. When an animal dies and leaves good friends there, they sense a difference since its departure, but their brains can't register this with a reason, and no images of their buddy are in their minds. Once the others start arriving here, they will be drawn to that first friend and eventually to all in their group because of the bonds they established there.

S: Do animals have memories during their lifetimes here of their good or bad experiences?

MATTHEW: Not explicit, graphic memories such as you do, but a memory energy. Let us say that a dog was severely abused and neglected for a year in its first home, then came into a family who cared for it conscientiously and kindly the rest of its life. If the dog developed behavior problems in puppyhood due to its traumatic experiences, the effects of that maltreatment remain lifelong in the dog's memory energy and are evident as its behavior. It is the deepest core of the brain cells that are affected, and the natural reactive behavior does not need to be accompanied by actual memories. However, the behavior may be softened if the dog receives only loving treatment in its second home. This cause-and-effect pattern is true of all animals.

I should add that work like yours, finding caring families for homeless dogs, is helping to strengthen the entire light network. Those animals who had been living in fear or deprivation no longer are emanating the negativity that their former circumstances were causing.

I know you feel guilty because your primary interest is helping dogs even though you see great need elsewhere for assistance, too. You are inspired to do what you are doing just as others are inspired to relieve human suffering or preserve endangered species or clean up the environment. All these types of assistance are invaluable in dispersing negativity or transmuting it into the light energy that is preparing Earth for her ascendance into a higher dimension.

ANGELS, SPIRIT GUIDES

S: Are you an angel now, Matthew?

MATTHEW: Mother, what a question! Goodness, NO! Angels are not the same as discarnate humans, although some of us are given that distinction without deserving it. Angels are collective energies of light, not a multitude of individual human beings, which we are. However, they can divide their energy into separate streams with personage characteristics for greater experiencing and purposeful missions, just as other collective souls can. They live in a different kind of placement from ours and their only purpose is safeguarding, assisting and comforting wherever it is needed. Also unlike human beings, the angels never separated from the Oneness spiritually.

But there are similarities between the angels and us. They have levels in their realm just as we do, with the return to Creator as our common bond and goal. And, when in personage, both they and we are in etheric bodies. But, also like us, they aren't always in their bodies. For instance, they are in spirit when their energy is with those who need help but wouldn't believe it if they saw an angel form. They also communicate telepathically just as we do, and they are alerted of the need for their services in the same way we are, by energy connections.

Just as we have responsibilities and learning to accomplish in our soul growth, so do the angels have theirs, through vigilance and assistance to their assigned souls. Generally, they have much more active participation in your lives than we do. Our spiritual contact with you is only by invitation, through your thoughts of us, whereas the angels are on constant duty to assist you.

And, neither they nor we have wings! Some accounts of dramatic rescues report angelic figures with wings. On those occasions the energy is so intense that the people manifest an atmosphere where they do see the angels' etheric bodies. In those times the angels may don wings if they wish—because they certainly can do that—but the expectations alone of people in such emotional straits can allow the perception of wings when none exist.

S: Does the energy frequency change when people are in great need, and that's what calls an angel to them?

MATTHEW: The *anticipation* of need is conveyed by energetic streams to the angels and they position themselves at the ready. Some people know when an angel is waiting nearby because angels' presence is marked by a brilliant aura discernible to those who are sensitive to energy fluctuations.

Many people in life-threatening situations have been saved by angels' intervention in accordance with those souls' chosen paths. However, if the dire circumstances are within the course of the souls' chosen lifetimes, the angels cannot interfere. When people are living in horrible situations or die violently, it doesn't mean that angels are not with them during those extreme times, but rather that the angels must respect the souls' chosen lessons which include those experiences. These angelic emissaries of God provide spiritual comfort, enlightenment and gentle guidance within your pre-birth choices, but they do not make decisions or give directions. Even though they are closer to you insofar as knowing details of your actions, thoughts and problems, they are no more permitted to interfere in your free will choices than are your families here.

However, angels are permitted to relieve mental or emotional anguish so severe that the human mind can no longer function rationally. This is not interference in those lives, it is within the province of compassion and sound judgment. Such expressions as "losing control" or "being out of your mind" are correct in those times, because the angels are taking over during the lapses. They provide the godly free zone between humans' rational and irrational functioning. If there were no angelic buffer between controlled behavior and desperation, or between miscalculation and its results, many physical lifetimes would be much shorter than the longevity clause in their pre-birth agreements.

S: What if death at that stage of a lifetime isn't part of a pre-birth agreement but the person does die, say in a massive earthquake or war or as a victim of a tyrannical regime that kills by the thousands? Surely not all those who die that way chose to, so why aren't a host of angels saving those lives?

MATTHEW: Mother, it is true that many soul contracts are being cut short by the situations you mentioned, and by others as well. And I know it's natural to think that since this is so, angels are not performing their assignments diligently. However, in this time of such accelerated happenings in the universe, not only on Earth, the end of physical lifetimes prior to agreement fulfillment is seen as providential. Many souls are choosing to leave Earth early to better prepare for ascendance to higher density spiritual evolvement here rather than remain there in insufferable conditions of fright, persecution, severely damaged bodies and other traumas associated with Earth in her present state. I assure you that the angels are not forfeiting their right and not abdicating their responsibilities regarding life-preserving, but are seeing the picture from this higher vantage point and in other ways are aiding the light forces' resolution to all of Earth's travails.

S: Our world is a mess, and I can't blame those people for wanting to move out early. Do you have anything else to tell me about angels?

MATTHEW: Yes, I can tell you more. Many of them function as free agents, not designated to a particular person, and often they are called upon to help an assigned angel in need of reinforced energy or wisdom. Indeed, angels are strong in energy and rich in wisdom, but even they have their limits! Often angels work through entities in human form who are, however, more than human in capability, and through them the angels perform their services. Also, some of the lower angelics can live within Earth density. They take on a human form and serve the needs of humanity with great benevolence. Someone who says, "She is an angel," might be absolutely right.

Angels visit here, but none are on assignment because there's no need for their protection and guidance, unlike on Earth where there is massive need for their extraordinary services. But they do benefit us in a different essential way. The music that motivates the expression "choirs of angels" is from energy vibrations sometimes ascribed to the flutter of angels' wings. Despite the actual wingless form of angels, that credit still is appropriate because they are in charge of the sounds of the spheres.

The angel assigned to each individual is known as that person's guardian angel, or gatekeeper. Every person, regardless of his belief or disbelief in angels' existence, has a guardian angel as his primary, constant, unseen, silent protector, helper and guide.

S: Aren't angels also called spirit guides?

MATTHEW: Sometimes, but not correctly. They aren't the same. Spirit guides are the spontaneous and temporary helpers who provide specialized advice or assistance. They are discarnate souls who have had many lifetimes in human bodies and can comprehend mortal needs, temptations and problems more easily than the higher angels, who have never known the limitations of the physical condition.

For instance, if you are baffled by a complicated appliance, a guide with electronic knowledge is reached energetically by a little "Help!" call that arises in your psyche and is transmitted to the ethers for an energy match. Obviously, that's not in the same league as a life-threatening situation to which your guardian angel would respond, but the "Oh, *now* I see" help still is welcome.

Mother, I'll give you real examples of recent help you've received. When you're stumped for a good transition to integrate segments of related material, your consternation reaches a soul here who has extensive writing experience— and, *voila,* you have it! It came from your guide for that specific moment's need. When you suddenly realize the material you're working with has a gap, you're responding to my nudge for a mini-sitting so I can amplify the subject. The light that I've told you is being focused on your work to lead it to publication originates from a multitude of sources in this realm and beyond.

On a more dramatic level, think back to that frightening near-accident soon after you learned to drive. Your guardian angel, Gregory, called for angels to assist him in dematerializing the car and you and your friends a split second before the crash would have happened. When it was safe, they transmuted the energy of you and your friends back into your normal density and the car back into its normal mass—they *re*-materialized you all.

S: That's astounding, Matthew! I've always thought I was in shock and that's why I couldn't understand why we didn't crash. It still stuns me that you know so much about my life, especially things like that, that I haven't thought about for decades. With all those willing helpers we have, do we ever do anything important by ourselves?

MATTHEW: Of course you do, but you also have far more help than you realize. There is no separation of the soul from any of the assisting forces—angels, spirit guides, beloved ones in this realm, light beings in other realms, God. Whatever help you require, even without consciously asking, or that which you earnestly request for yourself or someone you love, that need is registered in the same divine communication system open to all. Whether silent or verbalized, and regardless of to whom directed, your urgent cries for help reach God. Instantaneously the auxiliary lines of energy waves are directed appropriately for the circumstances and immediate help is provided.

The help may not always be recognized, though. Perhaps you pray fervently for the recovery of a beloved friend, yet she dies. Your plea for her recovery wasn't ignored, it was preempted by her pre-birth agreement. The response to your prayer could be more emotional strength and solace than if you hadn't prayed.

PRAYER

S: What is considered there to be a "proper" prayer?

MATTHEW: If such can be called "proper," your thoughts and feelings of love and caring for others are prayers. These can be at any time, in any place, with any words or no words, only feelings. The effects of prayer are directly related to the intent and intensity of the thoughts and feelings.

S: Are the effects of prayers diminished if the people don't go to church even though they know the value of group energy?

MATTHEW: God never meant churches to be buildings of any kind. The magnificent cathedrals are man's idea, not God's. Church is all within the soul. Church is one's feelings of reverence, of thanksgiving. It is the uplifting of the spirit into the love and light of God. In this way, church is a single prayer that has the ability to touch the universe.

In a church building filled with praying people, there may be only a few whose prayers have a pure and forceful energy flow. Many people pray with only a faint ritual observation, with no real energy. Others pray in such extreme distress or anxiety that their energy is distorted and has an adverse effect upon themselves as well as adding to universal negativity. Smooth energy flow is what positively affects each soul and the universe, not frenzied praying about specific conditions. It is *energy balance* that sustains and comforts.

I'm not speaking about the *intent* of the prayer, but only about the *effect* of the energy involved in the praying. The energy put forth in a prayer for a completely selfish, greedy purpose may be just as intense as a prayer put forth for the safety of a beloved family member or friend. The intent is recorded as one aspect and the energy flow, or force, is recorded as another.

Furthermore, one who prays for a specific outcome regarding another doesn't know that soul's pre-birth agreement. Conditions or events the pray-er is petitioning to have changed may be exactly those the soul chose as his life's lessons. The same is true of prayers for oneself, because your consciousness is rarely in communication with your soul. So pray for your own or another's *highest good* and don't direct intense emotion toward a specific outcome of your choosing. The outcome is NOT your conscious choice. You can feel a sense of relief in this knowledge, which will be registered in your sensitivity as peacefulness. That allows energy to proceed unencumbered not only within your physical and psychic self, but issued forth as harmony into Earth's consciousness.

Mother, I know you have heard that prayers "for the dead" are important and you've wondered why that would be necessary. Well, we aren't "dead," but since that reference is to souls in this realm, I want to assure you that prayers for us are indeed important. I don't mean only for those who arrive with great needs for comforting and healing, but also for us whose lives are vital and vibrant, with on-going lessons and spiritual growth. *Of course we need and welcome your prayers!* And please know that they are especially welcome when in balanced energy, because those prayers are the most beneficial to us and to you, our beloved ones.

TIME

S: You've said that time doesn't exist there as we know it, so why do you use the word "time" or refer to our specific time periods? Just please explain to me the difference between your time and ours.

MATTHEW: Well, Mother, I'll try. As for using your "time" words, we have to use the measurements you have devised for comprehending your past, present and future so you'll understand our messages. There's no common frame of reference except your languages, which have no words for clearly explaining our "time," or distance in the universal sense, either. None are needed in your languages because you have no way to perceive reality beyond your sensory dimensions. So it's much easier for us, and certainly for you, if we use your words relating to clocks and calendars although they're not applicable here.

We do have a sense of chronology, however, which we express as "soul growth stages" or "experiencing passages" or "sequential series of events." The process of accomplishing growth goals is our measurement of what you call past, present and future. I know this is quite imprecise by your standards, not to mention confusing!

Obviously, your vocabularies can't have explicit words to define that which is unknown to you, and so we can only make our best efforts at describing approximations of life beyond your consciousness. Actually, you have few words that can accurately or succinctly describe all the situations or feelings that you and I discuss, Mother. Maybe that's why I ramble so much when I'm trying to answer your questions.

I'll give you examples of our words that permit more expressiveness with ease than yours. "Insulan" is the word that explains how we operate as individual souls within the universal body of interconnectedness. Our "virtuous" embodies your definition, but it is more than having fine and admirable qualities—it describes the angels, encompassing their strength of purpose, great accomplishment of learning and serving, and exalted essence that has added to their light. When we say "placenta," we mean the protector or the protected space in which we live and experience. Maybe that's why your definition of that word is what it is.

I know I digressed from "time," but did I satisfactorily explain why we use your words that relate to it?

S: Yes, thank you, dear. Do you have any sense of the passing of time periods—say, between the beginning and ending of a day or a week here, for instance? How do you know when a particular class or event will start?

MATTHEW: Although we have variations in the colors of our skies at intervals that could be considered like your daybreak and eventide, we don't have periods equivalent to your 24-hour days or 7-day weeks. And we have no need to mark the beginning or ending of any time frame that is simply "time passing." However, our public occasions such as meetings, classes, lectures, concerts and the like do start at a designated "time," and an energy shift announces these events with plenty of notice so those who want to attend can wrap up other activities. So we do have advanced awareness of scheduled events and a sense of "soon" or "later," but not a specific moment.

Although mathematical science offers proof that your time structure doesn't exist beyond your use of it, computations of a time/space continuum on a blackboard—which are incomprehensible to most of you—are still far more easily achieved than the actuality within your psyches.

S: Some people believe Earth was created only several thousand years ago. In the universal concept of time, could they be right and the scientists whose estimates run in the billions of years be wrong?

MATTHEW: Since everyone there is using the same measuring stick—that is, a 365-day year—I'd have to say that those who believe Earth to be only several thousand years old are not right. The evolutionary development of the planet and its life forms could not have happened as it did and still be scrunched into that short time frame of your years. However, since all of your time measurements—minutes or millennia—are fabricated to suit only your purposes, both of those estimated ages are useless on a universal basis. Mother, it isn't necessary for your thoughts to struggle further with this time thing. The understanding will come with residency here.

INTRAREALM COMMUNICATION

S: If you want to be with someone there, how do you let that person know?

MATTHEW: I think of him. Well, it's much more than a thought, or everyone here would be forever visiting each other if only a thought brought us together. Contact is the result of a *mutual* desiring of presence or communication. It's a special energy wavelength. Our individual energy vibrations are as distinctive as Earth fingerprints and a great deal easier to track because there's no mechanism involved.

If we're busy when someone thinks of us only casually, without urgency or intense desire, by means of a privacy shielding our personal frequency emits a signal equivalent to your telephone's busy signal. Or, we can simply not want to be disturbed! In either case, much like a message left on your answer machine, the call is registered by the existence of the thought that initiated the signal. It is a noninterference, or non-interruption mechanism on a frequency that can be turned on and off, like your radio. When the shielding is removed there is instantaneous connection between the caller and the intended receiver.

This system enables both complete personal privacy and a mass communication method, such as public notification that a lecture is about to begin. It's actually nothing more than you have devised by harnessing the same energy through technical means, but here the technology is inherent in the realm existence and no equipment is needed for transmission or reception.

We have an easy and foolproof means for taking a message to pass on to someone, like those I've given you to relay. The originator literally impresses his thoughts upon my energy system for direct transference into my pulsations for you to receive. This is a simple downloading function like a basic process of your computers.

S: That's beyond me, as I'm sure you know, but that's OK—obviously, it works. Do you ever speak aloud, or is all your communication by those thought processes?

MATTHEW: We certainly can speak audibly, but the majority of our personal and public communication is telepathic, or as you said, "thought processes." In classes and public meetings there may be a spoken message of welcome out of courtesy to recently arrived souls who still are more comfortable with speech. The spoken message is simultaneously translated into all Earth languages and delivered to the audience via appropriate sound waves. But generally the lecture or meeting itself would be presented telepathically.

S: But wouldn't translation be necessary for telepathic exchange, too?

MATTHEW: Yes, it is. A common ground for interpreting the thought impressions is achieved by a process similar to a system developed for interaction between your different types of computers and software programs. It is a synthesis of knowledge exchange that is inherent in our cellular memory, so it isn't something that has to be learned, only remembered. This capability extends to spoken languages, too. We have talked with visitors from beyond our galaxy using a communication mode into which all languages and dialects are fed and translated instantaneously.

S: Matthew, do you ever talk with God?

MATTHEW: Yes, Mother, we do "talk." It is not what you would consider a real conversation, though, because far more than an exchange of words happens. It is an entire essence experience, one that I wish I could describe to you, but it isn't possible because your language doesn't have the words to explain it. The best I can do is tell you the sensation is like being melted into such encompassing love that words are not needed, yet the complete ideas are exchanged. It is a more exalted experience than even the love expressed among souls here that I've described to you.

S: Does God ever talk to any of us?

MATTHEW: All the time, if you'd but listen instead of thinking, thinking, thinking. And in the conversations with you there are words, because that is your form of communication and you wouldn't understand a message without words, would you?

COMMUNICATION WITH EARTH

S: Do you know everything that happens on Earth?

MATTHEW: All the events you could call public as opposed to private, personal events, yes. We see them occurring, we see the thoughts behind them, and we see the darkness or the light around both the events and the thoughts. Trained observers are assigned to monitor all happenings so that when help is needed and is within the pre-birth agreements, assistance can be rendered instantly.

S: I know from our sittings how quickly telepathic communication can happen and I'm wondering how you protect your private thoughts.

MATTHEW: Mother, what you're wondering is how the swiftness of telepathy affects *your* private thoughts! There are two issues here. I've told you about the privacy shielding that protects us here from interruption unless there is mutual desire for contact. A feature of that same shielding allows our private thoughts to be undisturbed.

As for your privacy, we must be invited into your thoughts. When we are, contact is instantaneous. Now you're concerned about what constitutes the invitation. Universal law does. When I am in your thoughts intently or only "casually" lovingly, your energy reaches me and I respond. When your thoughts are solely on another interest or activity, including those of personal physical nature, then your frequency for receiving from this realm isn't operating. There's no way I could intrude, because your energy in those times is denser than when you're dealing on a higher spiritual level. The energy attunement of that higher level is required for communication between this realm and Earth. So you see, Mother, you do have complete privacy of thought and activity when you want it!

S: I'm very glad to know that, Matthew! "Hearing" probably isn't the best term for my end of our communication. How would you describe it, just telepathic?

MATTHEW: Well, "just telepathic" still is a wide range of communication with realistic and powerful effects. As you know, the receiving aspect enables individual voices with personal inflections to be as real as if they are being heard on Earth. Actually, there is sound, but your auditory range is so small that rarely does anyone hear us even when we're speaking right beside him.

There are other dimensions of telepathic communication you have experienced but just aren't attributing to it. Simultaneously with hearing me, you see my punctuation and underlined words or words in all capital letters that I want to emphasize, and you see the images we send. You feel the energy of Ithaca, Esmeralda and others as well as mine. You feel me hug you. Twice you have smelled the lovely fragrance I've sent. So you see, the energy of telepathy encompasses all of your senses except taste, and I don't think we're going to be able to manage that one.

S: You're right, dear, and I was being shortsighted in my question. What I really need is an explanation of how I receive your messages.

MATTHEW: It's an energy transfer. You "hear" my thoughts impressed upon your consciousness. The pulsing of my thoughts takes an actual form, a thought form, that makes an impression upon your clean, receptive brain waves. The energy source is light that is electrically switched to pulses that are transferred at your level into your word vibrations. The pulses don't start out as words, but as vibratory rates indicating intelligence blips. There is continuous interaction, but always my thoughts precede your comprehension. My thoughts trigger words stored in your memory, and my thoughts carry a coding for choice. When your word is suitable for my purpose, I accept it, but when it's not, I correct it—as you know!

S: Matthew, I don't understand a word you said except that when I goof, you get on my case. Betsy asked me how our communication works, and she probably won't understand your energy transfer and pulsing explanation any more than I do. Can't you simplify it?

MATTHEW: Give me a moment to think, please. . . . Thank you.

Betsy, I shall give you an analogy of how I communicate with Mother. Consider a tire tread as my thought and the smooth soft earth as Mother's consciousness, or receiving area. Imagine the clear impression of the tread upon the earth. The tread mark is my thought impression upon Mother's consciousness.

Think of rain as Mother's vocabulary, and imagine some of the rain falling into the grooves of the tread marks, filling the space up to the level of the earth around those marks. The rain doesn't change the form of the impression, it only fills the space. That filled space can be considered my message, my thoughts filled with Mother's words that were appropriate for conveying my meaning.

Occasionally there is a slight extra impression in the grooves, say where a pebble is, and it causes a tiny deformity in the otherwise perfect tread mark. It's in those tiny degrees

*of deviation that my thought impression and Mother's vocab-
ulary produce a word that isn't my choice. When my intent
isn't changed by that word, no harm is done. In fact, it's not
up to me to choose every single word or we wouldn't finish
one message in a full day. But if Mother's word choice is
contrary to my meaning, I correct it.*

Mother, did I do all right on that analogy?

*S: Yes, thank you, dear! That makes it much more un-
derstandable. Sometimes I feel as if I'm thinking of all the
words being used, so naturally I wonder whether it's you or
I coming up with the information.*

MATTHEW: You don't interfere with my thought
forms by thinking of appropriate words, Mother. I don't
order up your words. You're responding to my pulsing by
making them available for my use. I depend upon your
words to fill in the grooves of my thought forms with sensible sentences that let you comprehend what I want to
convey. I pulse my intent through thought impressions,
and your energy, aided by your vocabulary, memory and
conscious assistance, lets the words that best express my
intent come to your mind. It seems to be simultaneous,
but there is an infinitesimal lag.

*S: Then why don't you speak the same way I would if
the intent is the same?*

MATTHEW: Because the pulsing is with *my* thoughts,
not yours! I need only your word reservoir, not your sequence
of words or your finite selection of words.

*S: Well, I never knew "evolvement" even existed, so where
did that come from?*

MATTHEW: Your familiarity with the syllables is enough.

S: OK. When we talk outside of sittings and I haven't prayed for protection as I do when I'm at the computer, am I still protected from dark energies?

MATTHEW: Absolutely you are! Everyone on Earth is totally protected during our communion with them! Many of us are simultaneously visiting or communicating with our beloved people there, whether you realize it or not, and to endanger any of you by seeking such contact is unthinkable, so automatically a protective shield is in force. When our energy connects with yours, the shielding is instantly wrapped around you, giving protection and communion passage. When the visitation ends, the shielding is withdrawn automatically as the energy connection dissipates, and our etheric bodies are then separate from the physical bodies of those whom we visited.

LOCATION

S: Where is Nirvana in relation to Earth?

MATTHEW: We're usually not much farther from Earth than your moon is, but this is not a static realm, so our relative positions vary. None of the other discarnate placements that serve the same purpose as Nirvana are static realms, either. We don't rotate as the planets do, and we aren't bound by the gravity that keeps your planetary system in orderly orbit.

S: I'm glad you're that close by! Is Nirvana a sphere or is it more like a planetary ring around Earth?

MATTHEW: I've never thought of this realm as a sphere, but it is more like that form than a ring. It has flexible boundaries, like an amoeba squirming before it divides. This realm is not a single place, but a *placement,* which means it can encompass various related, yet specific areas for experiencing. We have many layers of energy, and not all are connected. Our masters and Council members, who are the realm's highest souls in spiritual evolvement, live in the highest, or lightest density level. The other extreme is the lowest, or densest level, the layer where the lost souls live.

I know you have wondered how much is true of a book you read many years ago, which disturbed you because it described a form of hell that can be seen and visited on this plane where I am. Well, Mother, I know this because those concerns were so long a part of your thoughts about me, where I am and what it's like wherever that may be, and you didn't want to picture me even near such a place as you read about.

A hellish place such as that does exist as a part of Nirvana, but it isn't near this layer of the realm where I'm living. It is permanently removed from all of the other layers and never impinges upon our experiences. It couldn't possibly be near here because the conflict between the opposite energy densities would not enable its survival. The light here would lighten the darkness of that heaviest density layer, and the souls there have refused the light. Those unrepentant individuals are consigned to the darkness by their *self-judgment* review processes. They feel no guilt or remorse for pain they have knowingly, willingly and intentionally caused others.

On Earth all "evildoers" likely would be thought of as people who do unconscionable things, but in some cases, they lived according to pre-birth agreements for specific lessons to balance their energy fields. Others' actions that caused great pain and damage may have been dictated by mind control measures. And some do indeed make free will choices to deliberately hurt others. *Willful intent* is the energy registration that separates the last group from the others, and that is what consigns the people in that group to the lowest density layer of the realm.

S: Since their energy is so different from the energy of the rest of you, why do they live anywhere at all in Nirvana?

MATTHEW: Where else would you have them be, Mother? These are the souls of Earth humans who have made transition, not inhabitants of some other planetary system. In some cases, they recently were walking and working among you! They can't be sent simply "out there somewhere." If that were the case, they could do far greater damage than they can in a place of such density that escape is impossible by their own perpetuation. Furthermore, loving light energy is continually beamed to them by high beings, and if they respond to the light, they evolve into less dense layers of the realm.

I need to clarify something at this point. Energy, which is the life force of everything in creation, is *neutral.* It is the *intent,* or the directed use, of energy by souls that is the basis for our ascribing to it qualifications such as light, dark, base, positive, negative and so forth. Those qualities or conditions and all personal characteristics we classify as one's energy, or energy field, actually are energy *attachments,* but for simplicity, we drop "attachment" in ordinary references to the *effects* of energy usage.

S: I see. Matthew, please give me a minute to scroll back. Sometimes your information is so startling that not only can't I grasp what you're saying, I even forget my questions as I keep listening to you.

MATTHEW: I know you cannot carry two parallel thought patterns and do justice to either. That is the nature of these communications. There has to be your separation from the manual operation of recording to later permit the mental operation to come into play.

By all means, Mother, look back at my message. As I have told you, you may do whatever you wish during our sittings. Always! So may I, dear one, but never would I choose to do anything to disappoint you. The Matthew aspect of me would never permit that.

S: Does your Matthew aspect fluctuate in prominence or strength, or do all the lifetimes always have equal influence?

MATTHEW: It is not a matter of ascribing partitions

to the cumulative experiencing, with one compartment of the soul set apart from another. At this level there is a combining of all knowledge and all sensory experiencing of the cumulative lifetimes, and the intermingling is unavoidable. We would not want to avoid it, as most of the experiencing would be wasted and the chosen lessons would be needlessly repeated and repeated.

The thoughts and memories and sensory bonds that you correctly call a love bond are most prominent in the lifetime most recently experienced. So it is natural that when something you are thinking or feeling is at an intensity to reach me, my Matthew aspect rises in response. You have triggered this aspect. Still, even when the Matthew personage is most intensely connected with you, he encompasses experiencing of all lifetimes of this cumulative soul. As you are aware, you are not evoking the prominence of only the Matthew personage in this part of the discussion.

Now then, I believe you wanted to recapture your questions by reading a previous passage.

S: Yes, thank you. You said Nirvana has no regular orbiting. So what does hold you in space?

MATTHEW: There are what you might call disturbances that can be likened to cosmic dust storms which set in motion energy from available sources. These energies, which could be likened to an Earth cyclone or typhoon wind, have an orderly path that is in cooperation with rather than in opposition to themselves. This promotes movement that is quite dependable, not in its path but rather its velocity.

We are more in suspension than in orbit. The energies do not remain static in their path or even in this placement, but can move about the universe as if independent of other motions that normally would affect matter of greater mass than ours. I believe my example of an amoeba preparing to divide most aptly describes the movement path and flexibility of this realm, so if you can put such an image in the midst of your orbiting solar system, I believe you can envision the comparative movements of this realm and Earth.

S: OK, but now I'm going to see a giant amoeba in the sky when I think of you. The other thing I wanted to ask you is, how big is Nirvana?

MATTHEW: Now that's a lovely maternal image, Mother! Well, I suppose we could be compared to Venus in size, although any comparison to a sphere is not at all sensible because they don't have the flexibility and limitless expansion capacity we do. Our protective shielding has that expandable capacity, the universe has it, the entirety of Creation has it, but individual spheres don't.

S: What is that protective shielding you mentioned? Why do you have it?

MATTHEW: The shielding is a flexible blanket of light that permeates us, akin to your atmosphere in that it not only surrounds bodies, it is *within* them. We don't have the capability to fabricate this shield ourselves because it is made of substance and is more than our powers of manifestation can create. The shielding is the Christed light, radiant from Creator, transmitted to and through God and directed to our realm and the other realms that serve the same purpose as Nirvana.

The protection of the shield is necessary because we are close enough to Earth as to be otherwise severely affected by all the pollution and the interference from baser energies in the universe. Not those Earthbound energies, of course, but all others who wish to prey upon the sanctity of this realm.

The shield is powerful, almost impenetrable by entities less than our fourth density frequencies. I say "almost" because accidents have happened wherein the dark forces of higher dimensional advancement in technology, but not in spirituality, have pierced it and the baser energies have momentarily entered. But that is a rare occurrence and is discovered quickly, and no injuries can be caused to any residents or transients. That includes people from Earth who are visiting in dream state and those who experience the near-death supraconsciousness.

When there is a rent in the shield, there is a vibration of such force that Council members know immediately, and the warriors of the universe in the divine light of Christ service are on hand instantly, before more damage can be done to the shield or any significant numbers of base entities can enter.

It is puzzling to us why this combined force bothers, as those entities cannot live in this higher density and their energy is transmuted into our atmosphere. Their identities are lost, having served no lasting purpose. But they are merely tools of the dark forces, and life forms to them are expendable.

S: Are "base energies," "base entities" and "dark forces" synonymous terms for the same beings?

MATTHEW: Yes. Those terms and other similar ones are descriptive references that can be used interchangeably to designate the universally powerful force with the negative nature you commonly call evil.

"Dark" or "darkness" indicates entities that are operating far from the light. Their aim is to obliterate all light in Creation. "Base" energies or entities is descriptive of the level of density into which these beings have fallen away from God and Creator. Never are they separate from God and Creator in actuality, but in their limited light they are unaware of that reality.

The denser, or baser, the energy, the more negatively bound are the souls operating at that level. The basest placement of all, that bottom level of this multilayered universe, is the most distant from the angelic realms, which are at the highest, or lightest, level closest to Creator.

S: Matthew, I'm glad to know it's safe where you are! Who protects you before the shield is repaired and who repairs it?

MATTHEW: Usually members of Hatonn's intergalactic force do both. A segment of his fleet, which generally is based in the Pleiades system, is in space as guardians of the shielding here and in the other realms like ours. They also maintain the shield in its natural state of total protectiveness.

The crew is not exactly in charge of protection for this realm, but they have become the main watchers of disturbances in the past several years while they've been so prevalent in this area. Thousands of these small spacecraft are on patrol around here at any one time. They rotate on this guard assignment much the way police patrols do on Earth. Prior to their taking on this responsibility, a large spacecraft from Sirius usually was nearby or made frequent stops to monitor our shield.

S: Have you met any members of the repair crew?

MATTHEW: I've met some of them and have thoroughly enjoyed the exchange of ideas and information. One of my favorites comes here occasionally just to visit me, not to do any work. He admires the pace and variety of my life and says his visits here are like holidays because it gets boring just flying around the universe all the time.

S: I suppose every job gets dull after a while. How do they repair the shield?

MATTHEW: The repair process is essentially holding the energy stable, or anchoring it at the gap in the shield, then pulling energy from another source and harnessing it at the velocity and frequency required to unite the two energy paths. Energy has its own glue, but it has to be manipulated into proper position and superheated, which is why velocity is accelerated to achieve the fusion required.

S: Do the repair crews come in physical bodies?

MATTHEW: Usually they come in their fourth density human bodies, but they don't have to. They can manifest handsome bodies once they're here because our light atmosphere permits that without entrapping them. Third density bodies, which yours are, can't enter this realm, and that's why only your souls come on visits.

S: Please tell me more about those forces that can penetrate the shield.

MATTHEW: They're the dark forces that want to disrupt the tranquility, learning and healing, and especially the spiritual evolution, that go on here. We're constantly fighting these foes—not in battle as you think of it, with fighting forces and weapons, but with light. Often these energies are an unidentifiable entity. A force field probably is a better designation, and it is powerful. Mother, there are activities of such massive destruction on the inner planes that they are beyond your comprehension. Sometimes it is beyond my own, not as to what is happening, but why.

The entire universe is being affected by this era of upheaval. The corruption and deceit and warmongering on Earth are not the cause of catastrophic world events there, but *symptoms* of the wider spread and more drastic events happening on a universal scale. In many ways we are protected from the harshness that is affecting so many other souls.

However, we aren't just a little patch of protected beings, nor are the other sanctuary realms. There is a reason for our stability in the face of furor around us, just as there is a place for the one wise, calm being to remain in balance even while surrounded by turmoil. Nirvana and the other realms of greater purity and clarity are grounding points for the universe, stabilizing elements essential for holding the revolution of solar systems on a stable course. The force field of spirituality prevailing in these areas of higher density is in a constant rate of stability.

The dependable harmony, peacefulness and stability of our higher density can be relied upon without exception to be a fulcrum for the balancing of external elements. This is true regardless of the influx of souls, because there is immediate assignment in accordance with the transitional energy that reflects each soul's Earth lifetime activities. You could say that this stability is the "Heaven" of Nirvana because the part that could be considered the "hell" doesn't have it.

TRAVEL

S: You've mentioned that travel is one of the major activities of Nirvana residents, and of course I know you come here. How do you do that, and where else do you go?

MATTHEW: Mother, travel is constantly going on here! Our privacy shielding keeps the activity of millions of travelers within the realm, and all those who are coming or leaving here at any given moment, from bothering anyone else. Otherwise, it would be Pandemonium here.

For travel within the realm, we have the same kinds of transportation you do. People who enjoy driving or flying or boating or taking train or bus rides manifest those vehicles as they want them. We have other modes as well, but probably the most common of all is astral travel in a body less dense than our everyday etheric bodies. The astral body permits travel almost anywhere—well, anywhere light beings would want to go—and although it is an awesome experience, it's not without risks. There are universal highways, so to speak. Astral travel is limited to a spectrum of wavelengths within a defined band that enables this travel with ease. Outside that band either it's dangerous to the frequency of the discarnate soul or it isn't compatible at all and therefore not even a possibility. Most folks on Earth cannot fathom that space travel in such different modes and speeds is happening constantly throughout the universe—within or without spacecraft!

There are frequent visitations between here and the other discarnate realms. They differ from Nirvana because their residents in physical lifetime lived in considerably different environments from Earth's, and each world's spirit realm is designed to best accommodate the souls who reside there. Most of those realms are not nearly as beautiful as Nirvana, even though they may be further advanced technologically. Our master teachers often come from those placements specifically to instruct us in the technology that we then make available in the ethers for accessing by scientists and engineers on Earth.

I have visited many of the other haven realms within this galaxy, but I don't often go to those in other galaxies. This isn't due to lack of interest, but purely for the need of my services here. It's the same as your taking a long vacation far away when your responsibilities permit that, and when they don't, you take a short break close to home. For us it isn't the distance involved, it's the complexities of density and other aspects of astral travel that discourage my trips beyond this galaxy. For that same reason, except to Earth, I rarely travel to places with physical inhabitants. The vibratory rates are different and a great deal of preparation and recovery effort is required for travel to many of those placements.

S: I read somewhere that the density of Earth can trap evolved life forms who come here in physical bodies. If that's so, why, and what happens to them?

MATTHEW: What you have read is correct. Materializing for entering a lower density is much easier than raising that density to a level that is safer for the traveler. Energy is the means by which the densities are changed and the means by which the transport is accomplished. The combination is the risk element. Becoming trapped in the lower density and losing all former universal awareness all too often is the outcome for those who make such journeys, so wisdom decrees that when such travel is undertaken, the mission be accomplished with all haste and the leave-taking be prompt.

S: But you can come here in your etheric body and not be trapped. What allows that difference?

MATTHEW: The safety of our higher frequency bodies is assured by our protective shielding. At one time Earth had no more density than Nirvana—that's why there could be continuous travel back and forth. Now we must have a blanket of light energy to protect us from the negativity that creates the density of Earth. This negativity is what caused the end of the former total ease of passage and constant telepathic communication between our two worlds.

We don't venture into densities lower than third without special purpose, protection and mission clearance from Council. The purpose would be a service of utmost love, perhaps to a beloved one who had fallen so far from the light that a concerned soul here asks to assist in a recovery request. The request may be initiated either by the fallen soul or by one who petitions for assistance on behalf of that soul.

RECREATION

S: Do you have any recreational activities like ours other than travel? Well, much more like ours than your travel!

MATTHEW: In many cases we do, but with some differences, as you might imagine. Sporting events are very popular here, just as they are there, but we consider sports to be as much learning experiences as recreation, and our attitude about team sports differs from yours. Those of us who share the same game interests are a group of friends rather than an organization such as your teams are. No people are excluded because they're not as proficient as others, and naturally, no players get exorbitant salaries. And there's no spirit of "Kill 'em!" in our competitions!

We have a multitude of other sports, too, for individuals or a few people sharing the activity. There's swimming, which is still my favorite of all, and tennis, golf, cycling, all of your winter sports—actually, we have all the sports you do except those that damage or destroy any kind of life. That includes boxing, which can injure the brain, and of course we don't have hunting, fishing or any kind of animal fights. But those types of activities aren't missed by the people who had been attracted to them as participants or spectators on Earth. Once they see the sanctity of ALL life here, they easily switch their interests to nondestructive recreation. Oh, and we don't engage in stupid things like mud wrestling or "chicken" driving, either.

Entertainment is a huge part of our recreation here, just as there. Our concerts are magnificent! Some sound like 10,000 stringed instruments and flutes and reeds in angelic purity. We have other types of concerts, too, with music so beautiful that all who attend are enthralled. But, if we choose not to be at the concert site, we can be wherever we wish and tune into the radio wave that corresponds to the emanating source and we don't miss a note.

Dramatic productions are immensely popular and their caliber exceeds even your most spectacular shows. In our theaters, just as in our concert halls, we have those exceptionally talented people who once performed so brilliantly for you. We have great writers whose works still thrill audiences there, and Broadway and Hollywood actors and actresses so admired on Earth. Without the limitations of their former third density world, their performances are finer than any ever seen there. We have the people "behind the scenes" too, whose masterful technical or artistic talents are essential parts of any splendid show. The theaters themselves are dramatic showcases, and our "special effects" surpass your imagination—you could say literally, the sky's the limit!

There's a more intimate entertainment form that we call simply "story hour." Our storytellers are so expert that they enchant adults as well as children, so these events are popular, too. So are large or small social gatherings of people sharing mutual interests, just as you enjoy, but no alcohol or "social" drugs are ever served at our fiestas.

All of those are important parts of life here, but our recreation can be as simple as a short, pleasant conversation or seeing an enchanting view. Charming moments such as those are not regarded on Earth with the recognition and appreciation they deserve for uplifting the spirit, which is what *re-creation* is all about.

Also, learning is such a pleasure for us that public lectures and guest speakers in a class are a type of recreation, and on Earth very few folks consider classrooms to be recreational places.

S: I can stop wondering if you have enough to do there. Do you have television?

MATTHEW: Not generally, but those newly arrived folks who so greatly enjoyed watching television during Earth lifetimes can manifest their own sets if they want to. The programming might be limited, though, as they also must manifest that! Our exchange of talent into entertainment is live, and it's such superb quality and variety that, once adjusted to life here, hardly anyone prefers "mechanical" entertainment.

All who want to attend the concerts or theatrical productions may do so. No high ticket prices prevent attendance, and there are no bad seats. Seating space isn't a consideration either because we don't have to contend with dense physical bodies. Transportation isn't a problem, either. Arrival can be instantaneous, because only the desirous thought of going is necessary, and there are no shut-ins due to physical constraints. If people there had the same easy means of attending live performances we have, I think far fewer folks would spend so much time in front of TV sets, don't you?

S: I'd certainly think so! Do you celebrate any of our holidays?

MATTHEW: We reverently acknowledge the most sacred days of all the religions represented here, but those various times may be more actively celebrated by individuals whose journey was in accordance with their chosen religion during their immediate past lifetime.

Mother, because of their relevance in this context, I want to mention again two things I've told you. First, we are cumulative souls, not only the soul of the last lifetime, and most of us have experienced many lifetimes in the various *godly* religions of Earth—so have most of you. I specify "godly" because Satanism, however UNgodly, is classified as a religion there—and no Satanist would ever be here! Second, the *soul energy* of the most holy figures of Earth's major religions came from the Christed realm, that highest angelic realm closest to Creator. With that same origin, none can be considered more enlightened or holy than any other.

National holidays on Earth are not celebrated as such here, but we are well aware of the pomp and ceremony there. We observe the parades and speeches with both humor and sadness because of the political deception behind it all. No, Mother, I don't want to get into a discussion of your politics now, so please dismiss your question!

BUILDINGS

S: Are your buildings like ours in size, appearance and construction, or totally unlike anything I'd recognize?

MATTHEW: You would have no trouble at all recognizing our buildings, Mother, but you would look at them in amazement because they *glow!* The construction materials are discarnate substances whose density encompasses a glowing frequency. However, there is considerable difference in the luminous intensity of the buildings.

All public buildings glow more than residential ones, but there are degrees of luminosity in both types of structures. The homes of our masters and Council members glow more than any others, and it has nothing to do with size or style, only with the occupants. That same variance is true of our multiresident apartment buildings.

The extent of emanated light in public buildings is determined by their intended use, which in turn determines the thought processes required for their design and erection. Manifesting huge, elaborate buildings with exalted purposes requires immense amounts of increasingly controlled power. The process of manifesting them doesn't take much time, but the arrangements that enable that process to happen involve extensive cooperation and intricate planning by our large force of expert architects and engineers.

Our grand hall, which surpasses your largest arenas and majestic cathedrals in size and grandeur, could be considered the crown jewel of all structures throughout this realm. Its gleaming essence will forevermore reflect the light not only of its marble and gold, but also of the energy that accomplished its design and construction. Erecting this magnificent building required thousands of souls working in tandem, with their minds focused in directing energy into specific areas. But before that could happen there was a lengthy time of concentrating their powers in planning and designing the features that later would be visualized into form. We have many other spectacular public buildings, too, and depending upon size and style, the erection of each required correspondingly fewer souls and less planning energy than the grand hall.

Now, as for residences, we have many large multiple-residence buildings with plain or luxurious apartments that can comfortably accommodate several individuals. These buildings are similar to yours, but even the smallest and simplest are much more appealing than those you call tenements. Our architectural designs include features for fine design, privacy and cheerfulness, and the landscaping always is beautiful.

Since far more single souls are here at any one time than mates or families, there are many huge, attractive dormitory-type buildings. Most are near the center, where colleges and lecture halls and other central civic activities are housed. Single souls also may choose private houses, of course.

Every residence size, architectural style and construction materials that can be visualized are available, from little two-room houses to pretentious manors that require 50 or more souls to plan and erect. Or, people may live in a rustic cabin in the mountains or on a ship or at a campsite in the woods, if any of those living quarters appeal to them.

So, you can see that our neighborhoods vary considerably, just as they do on Earth, but in this part of the realm there's no dirt or trash or decay anywhere. Even slums would have to be manifested, and no one here would choose to do that, so everything is pristine and orderly, and all private and public buildings are maintained in excellent condition. We don't consider any neighbor poor, and there's no "wrong side of the tracks."

S: Can people choose whatever kind of house and location they want?

MATTHEW: It's a bit more involved than that. There's no ownership, as in deeds and legal documents for assuring clear and uncontested title, and naturally, no monetary restrictions. But there is an earning basis for all housing accommodations. It is a system of self-evaluation, both of one's service during the Earth lifetime and the spiritual growth here, combined with Council recommendations for motivation and progress. As one progresses in selected learning, a move to finer living quarters is possible, but it's not required. Our most evolved souls often choose a simple little house rather than the fine estates to which they're entitled.

All of our public buildings and apartment houses are manifested by the highly skilled construction workers, and most people request their professional help in the design and manifestation of their homes. The services of this specialized field are made available to everyone, but some individuals choose to build their own houses. Small, uncomplicated structures can be planned and erected by as few as two nonprofessional builders who have studied the principles of construction. At least two souls, regardless of training, are required at this realm's level of manifesting capability.

S: Why? Since you can manifest whatever weather you want, I'd think that manifesting a simple little house would be a snap.

MATTHEW: A comparison of manifesting weather and a building is like your figure of speech "comparing apples and oranges." Manifesting weather uses elements in ready form. Manifesting buildings requires not only a more complex visualization process, but also the creation of the construction materials.

Mother, I'll explain why it takes at least two of us to manifest even a tiny building. Think of a flattened cardboard carton. Its two "walls" abut the fold lines—that's the shape building you would get if only one soul were manifesting it, and it would be worthless. To achieve a useful building requires, simultaneously, one mind visualizing the exterior specifications and another mind focusing on a detailed vision of the interior, and that combination gives the house a functional form.

S: I see, but I'm still surprised by that limitation of manifesting ability there.

MATTHEW: Mother dear, this placement does not offer the zenith of attainment that you still think it does. No soul here has sufficient concentration momentum to erect by himself even the simplest, smallest building. We're in a learning and growth mode, just like you. This realm offers more advanced courses than Earth can, but our capabilities in any field are less than those same types of capabilities in higher density beings. We are fourth density level humans, so you can see that both the intelligence and manifesting capability of souls in the sixth and seventh levels far exceed ours.

I know you have heard both "density" and "dimension" used to indicate levels of evolvement. The terms are meant to be the same, but density is the more correct because it is a description within the context of natural laws of vibratory rates, and dimension has no such defining characteristics.

Other placements may be the same or even higher than we are in soul evolvement, intelligence and technology, but they may use lower density construction materials. For instance, fourth density humans living in physical bodies may construct their buildings and spacecraft of materials whose molecular structures can be seen with your third density vision. That is in keeping with their own existence in *form*. It also is why their spacecraft can be seen from Earth.

S: I'm confused about this density thing. Why can I see a fourth density spacecraft and I can't see your fourth density body when you're right here with me?

MATTHEW: It is the difference of the *form* only, and not the level of spiritual or intellectual evolvement. Part of the confusion comes from this, Mother—you have only two designations for a state of being, either physical bodies and solid structures or no visible form at all. Since your third density vision can't see any body except a physical one, you consider this realm to be without form, or, "discarnate."

This *is* a discarnate placement with discarnate souls, where everything is done in discarnate fashion. The error is in your interpretation of discarnate, which you consider as life without form or substance. That definitely is *not* the case with us, as you've seen for yourself in the images we send you. But since you have only two concepts as your options, then describing us and this realm as discarnate is more accurate than any term indicating solid. So, just as we use "time" within your concept of it so you can understand our explanations, we use "discarnate" for describing all sanctuary realms and residents to distinguish us from those individuals and placements whose composition is solid.

S: Thank you for explaining that. Back to manifesting, please—I still don't understand how you can make something out of "thin air."

MATTHEW: The power of manifestation is not known on Earth, so it's no wonder that you don't understand it. That explanation I gave you some time ago was terrible, and I'll try to do better this time. As a process, manifestation is making something by first visualizing exactly what you want and then amassing and directing sufficient thought form energy to produce a substantial form identical to your image. Everything of substance, everything of the surroundings, every aspect of a soul's activities here and on Earth—*everything everywhere!*—is put into effect by the magnitude of power these energy-directing thought forms impart.

S: Matthew, thank you, that's enough for now. This has been a long sitting and before we end it, I want you tell me where you live.

MATTHEW: That I'd love to do! I live in one of the large dormitory-type buildings with apartments designed for the comfort and convenience of one person. No kitchen is needed because food is manifested to desired "doneness" without the need for a stove, so in this building each apartment has only two rooms, a public area and a private area. Mother, since you're wondering if I couldn't have a house after all the time I've been here, yes, I could, and quite a nice one, but I prefer an apartment for now, and mine suits me perfectly.

The basic color is shiny white and the current accent colors are spring green and brilliant gold and yellow tones. It's like sunshine caught in every inch of this place. Well, I'll *show* you! . . . You're receiving the image almost correctly, enough to recognize Frank Lloyd Wright's technique of light and shadow for wall decoration rather than pictures. He is a popular architect here.

My furniture is similar to your image, but it has simpler lines and is sturdier than you're seeing. There, now you have it exactly—*again!* Mother, for an instant you did get the image correctly, then you backed off because you felt you were *imagining* our family furniture instead of *seeing* mine. You're right, mine is almost identical to the furniture we had at home, and why not? I liked the style then and I still do.

I see you smiling at the bundles of live blossoms and tree branches in big vases throughout my rooms, so I believe I must have your approval in my decor. Well, since that was our family's decorating style and colors, my choices shouldn't surprise you.

S: I love it all, Matthew! You have created a gorgeous spring day to live in. It's so wonderful for me to be able to envision you in your own home! Thank you, dear! This means so much to me!

MATTHEW: I know it does, Mother, I can feel your excitement. And, you are more right on than you thought about my creating a vista of springtime. Remember, I told you we can manifest our private surroundings? I've chosen spring outside, too—not only the sunshine and warm breezes, but a whole springtime is outside my windows. You can see that right now I have a woodsy setting so that my view is similar to yours, but I can just as easily have a seashore, a formal garden, a field of cows or snowcapped mountains. Whatever scenery I can imagine, I can manifest.

S: It's all glorious, and I'm so pleased that you want the same kind of ambiente—*just a bit of Spanish there— as we had when you were here, and now even the woods, too. Since the views are what each person chooses, can anyone else see yours, or only you?*

MATTHEW: Anyone who wishes to peek into a private surrounding may do so, but usually that is by request, not a common occurrence, but if someone comes to my apartment, he automatically would see the same view from my windows as I. What casual passersby would see is the landscaping common to all residents of this building.

S: I see. Apparently everyone decorates inside according to personal taste, just as we do.

MATTHEW: Yes, and limitless choices are true of our furniture and all decorations, too. Everyone manifests whatever decor appeals at that time, and when they want a fresh look, redecorating can be virtually spontaneous. Mother, you'll have a ball here!

CULTURAL RESOURCES

S: Let's start where we left off yesterday, your build-
ings. Do you have art galleries or museums?

MATTHEW: We have both. Our galleries are among
our most impressive, spacious and glistening public buildings, and they're filled with art similar to that of your old
masters as well as your gifted modern painters and sculp-
tors. That glistening effect is heightened both by the art
treasures themselves and by the admiration of all who me-
ander through the buildings. Most galleries are designed
with display courtyards for visitors' additional enjoyment
as there's no danger to the art forms from changing weather.
No one would manifest a hurricane there!

Our museums are filled with treasures that on Earth
have been lost or destroyed through negligence and inten-
tional destruction. They have been recreated to commemo-
rate the cultures that produced them, and they aid in
teaching authentic Earth history. These items of rare worth
and beauty don't have to be behind glass with alarms for
safekeeping, of course, and touching by the millions of viewers doesn't damage them because the energy of admiration
and awe is pure and leaves no residue.

Some of the palatial homes are furnished with such
exquisite reproductions from eras when rulers of empires
reigned in opulence, you would think you were in a museum rather than a residence. Often that furniture does
wind up in a museum because rarely do the owners choose
to live very long in such pomp. Sometimes they manifest
those ornate pieces simply because they can, and that splen-

dor may have been part of a life they have known. But in time, most of those folks feel uncomfortable with that sort of conspicuous inequality because it's not in keeping with the realm's equality for spiritual growth and service. Then they either donate those regal trappings to museums or just unmanifest them.

S: You've mentioned studies and libraries, so I'm assuming you have textbooks and references of all sorts, classic literature and the holy books of all religions. Do those satisfy everybody's reading interests—here it wouldn't.

MATTHEW: Mother, our libraries are larger than any on Earth, and we have almost every kind of book you do except pornographic and those that could be called trashy. That isn't censorship, it's simply the manifesting choices of our residents, who may create whatever reading material they wish. We do have some books, though, that probably aren't thought of in conjunction with Heaven, like comics. Youngsters often ask if we have any, and if we don't have their favorites at hand, we manifest them because those help the little tykes adjust to their new life. We even have catalogues. Choosing and ordering items was a pleasant part of many people's life-style, and while they're becoming acclimated here, they still enjoy perusing those books. When they learn to manifest whatever they want, catalogues become a source of ideas.

Of course, you're right about the books you're "assuming" are here, and as for the holy books, we have all the editions of them. You're familiar only with the Bible, Mother, and you might be shocked to know that since the first writings, a great deal has been expunged or rewritten in subsequent versions. The original texts differ so greatly from today's version that there is no resemblance to the same numbered verses in the various revisions. All references that clearly indicated reincarnation and multiple lives for spiritual growth were deleted, which is why today's Bible differs in this respect from some other religions' holy books.

S: Why was the Bible changed?

MATTHEW: Those changes I mentioned were made to further the controlling aims of the few powerful people who had the authority and influence to amend the texts. In their view there was a need to separate the people from God, and since the first writings related the Oneness of all life, obviously those passages had to be changed so an authoritative layer of church hierarchy could be placed between the people and God. Money was a factor, too. The mentality of the early church hierarchy was political, and greed of all sorts motivated their instituting whatever ecclesiastical laws and philosophies would solidify their authority and control as well as enrich them monetarily.

S: Please give me an example of a change they made.

MATTHEW: I'll give you an example that is a wholly concocted addition—the story of God telling Abraham to sacrifice his son as proof that he loved God. That was fabricated purely to present the Almighty in that fearsome light, and it's considered one of the most unholy changes in biblical texts because it so distorts the totally loving nature of God. That story shows that God would command one of His own creations to kill another. God *never* would command a killing be done by anyone for *any* reason, much less as evidence that the killer sufficiently loved Him! And never did God wish the sacrifice of even an animal, because those creatures are His creations also. Animal sacrifices were not devised by God, but by the darkness in humankind.

The church potentates wanted the people to be afraid not to do whatever they decreed, so their decrees were presented in the name of God. That Abraham and Isaac story was contrived to show that God is to be feared and is no respecter of life unless the person obeys Him, which meant obeying the religious dogma devised by those potentates and levied on the populace.

There are many other strategic changes with the same basic motives. The full true message of Jesus is not within your Bible. His true message showed the truth of a loving God, the truth of the soul, the truth of this realm, the truth of the multilifetime spiritual journey to reintegration with Creator. His mission was to bring enLIGHTenment, to be the great teacher that many did consider him to be, to be God's messenger of Truth. Never was his mission to be the "king" that the devious church hierarchy tried to portray so they could dispose of him, eradicate his true teachings and introduce their own.

Unaware that the basis for many of today's religious doctrines is not the word of God through divinely inspired recorders, many of your churches are rooted in the dogma devised by those manipulative early church leaders. Eventually, with the acceleration of light being beamed at Earth from celestial beings helping your planet in her ascendance, both the truth and the falsehoods literally will "come to light."

JESUS

S: Matthew, have you ever seen Jesus?

MATTHEW: Oh, yes. Although he is in more demand than anyone else in this realm, I have been privileged not only to have seen him, but honored to have worked under his guidance.

Jesus is not a resident of Nirvana. He has the power to visit here in etheric body, to instruct, to nurture and heal, but he doesn't remain long at any one visit. He is everywhere in lighted space throughout this universe, although not known by the name Jesus—or Emmanuel, his given name. Although he often is referred to on Earth as Jesus Christ, Christ is not part of his name, but rather designates his Christed beingness. Christ is not a proper name. It means "being one with God," and it is just as correct to say "Buddha the Christ" as it is to say "Jesus the Christ."

Jesus is a creation of God and the Christed energy, that most pure, loving and high angelic station closest to Creator. The Christed energy is supremely respected and is all-powerful throughout this universe. Jesus' influence, benevolence and inspiration are needed in higher echelons as well as here, and they are very greatly needed on Earth. His message as perceived there is so limited that it is a dreadful travesty because his abilities in evidence of God's power and love are so much more profound than are attributed to him.

That same God fragment who embodied as Jesus has incarnated in other Earth lifetimes throughout human history. One such personage was Buddha, whose followers have kept his message more intact than Christianity's adherents have kept the message of Jesus. Other embodiments of the Christed energy have appeared in human form in other planetary systems, but not in the same religious leader status as Jesus and other major personages of Earth religions.

S: That is a great deal to contemplate, Matthew—it's so different from what we are taught. Do we regard the saints the same as you?

MATTHEW: I know how different the teachings are, Mother, but it is essential that the truth be known on Earth. In the case of saints, it is the reverse from your limited understanding of the powers of Jesus. The people designated as saints by the Catholic Church are honored here for their progression along the path of enlightenment, just as all other souls of high spiritual attainment are. However, that is less than the evolvement with which they have been endowed by the church. The church hierarchy strategically elevated individuals to sainthood to create another layer between the masses and God. Although the saints were indeed worthy individuals, that distancing ploy exalted them far above their pre-birth chosen missions and human capacities.

Throughout the centuries of religious influences, the people have suffered greatly due to that distancing and other "spiritual" control that religions have exercised over their lives. For many, adjustment to the reality of life in this realm has been made very difficult because of the dogma devised by the self-serving early church leaders that still is in effect today.

EDUCATION

S: You often mention soul growth and studying. I used to think that when our souls go to Heaven, automatically they are completely evolved and all knowledge is revealed. So, how far advanced in spiritual growth and learning are Nirvana's residents?

MATTHEW: Mother, residency here never has meant automatic soul advancement or automatic entry into universal knowledge. Remember that I told you it was created as a haven for the wounded souls in antiquity who needed to heal in a protected place? So you see, Nirvana wasn't designed to be the ultimate in knowledge or soul awareness, and it still isn't. The haven for wounded warriors is no longer the purpose, of course, so now this placement is only one more stage for learning, one more step along the path in soul evolution. Furthermore, just because I am here and you are there doesn't make the difference in our soul progression. Spirit lifetime is the same as physical lifetime insofar as lessons to be learned, and many people on Earth are further along in their soul evolution than many of us in this world.

No moment of existence *anywhere* is devoid of learning opportunities. This doesn't mean that a burdensome academic atmosphere exists in all moments of all lifetimes or that every soul must be interested in learning. It does mean that learning is movement toward the goal of all souls, reintegration with the Oneness, so it's natural that we put great emphasis upon taking advantage of all learning opportunities.

Even though this realm is not as dramatic a school as

Earth is, we have considerable advantages you don't have. Since we aren't constrained by your limitations of physical density, full usage of the brain and an accelerated rate of learning are possible. We aren't limited by your third density senses, either. Our access to learning resources is unparalleled, and there's a harmonious flow of energy that is both stimulating and uplifting within an educational environment.

S: Other than your advantages, is education there anything like ours?

MATTHEW: A great deal like yours. We have regular classes with books, professors who offer instruction in myriad subjects, guest lecturers, training tools and progress evaluation. Master orators and educators from higher density placements come to advance us in areas beyond abilities and knowledge common to this realm. Our immense libraries are complete reference centers with all the worthy reading and research material you have plus many other sources of information you've never heard of, such as records of Earth eras that are unknown to you.

Nothing prevents anyone from enrolling in any class he chooses. There's no such thing as a class being closed because it's too full and there's no requirement to take classes in ascending order, like your 101, 102 and so forth. Obviously there's no tuition, or any other limiting factor except one's own interest and enthusiasm. There's a learning curve proportional to the number in the class, the acceleration rate of assimilating the information, and the attitude of the students. Many students do have difficulty making the grade, but there are no Fs, and we all pitch in to help them with their studies. This form of tutoring, coming from personal interest and willingness, not only is helpful to the foundering students but also it's gratifying to those who assist them. Having no "time" is an advantage, too—no bells end class or study periods, and a student may stay as long as he wishes.

Some of our academic buildings are large and imposing, and others are like the mobile trailers you have to supplement regular classroom space. Except for the luminosity of all our buildings, our educational settings are very similar to your largest high school and university campuses.

S: All of that sounds like an ideal learning atmosphere.

MATTHEW: It is, but it does present a challenge to the lazy soul. It is not mandatory to study or grow, it is purely individual choice. There are no failing grades, no reprimands, no expulsion for absence to pressure people with borderline attitudes to wake up. Consequently, a life here can be wasted due to the lack of external motivation, and those who wait to be prodded into shaping up are out of luck.

And I'm not talking about learning only through formal education, Mother. I'm talking about all types of learning here, just as it exists there, where people also learn from their experiences and the experiences of others—the lessons of life. Laziness in learning is no more rewarded here than there, and when lazy souls leave here, their next lifetime is a backward move.

Although we can select the lessons we want, guidance is available in the Akashic Records, which reveal our experiencing and life lessons started but still incomplete. Heeding that guidance leads to the most sensible and beneficial preparation for the lifetime ahead, but still, we have total freedom to choose what we want to learn.

S: What academic courses are available?

MATTHEW: All the sciences, arts, languages, engineering—really, every one you can imagine from astronomy to mythology to zoology. Why mythology? Because it's fascinating to compare the revelations about antiquity with what we were taught on Earth. Unlike what is taught there, the legends of mythology are much more than ancient attempts to explain human existence and natural phenomena—most are accounts of actual happenings.

For instance, there really were those combination animal and human beings, but the truth is not nearly as frivolous as the stories of singing mermaids and piping goat-men and prancing centaurs. Those intelligent, miserable creatures were the manifestations of depraved minds with only self-serving interests in their cruel creation of such beings. Some were designed especially to do jobs that required the capability to think and perform labor that humans couldn't do, such as work underwater for long periods, or didn't want to do.

S: That's not at all a nice revelation to hear about. Matthew, is there usually such a difference in what you learn and what we're taught?

MATTHEW: It depends upon the field of study. Our medical studies go beyond those on Earth, yet they eliminate most of the medical education there. We don't need any training in broken bones or diseases because none of those are here, and we don't need pharmaceutical knowledge because we don't use "prescription" drugs.

Treatment is by directed energy vibrations, and all maladies of the newcomers are healed by this means. The physical body's memories are acute, and the immediate hold those memories have over the etheric body is profound.

We learn how to realign the energy so the discarded physical body leaves no lingering hold on the etheric body that will encumber or lessen its potential for fullness of living.

The same is true of a damaged psyche, which often goes hand in hand with the body's need for healing. So our psychology studies have the same focus, but here we go directly to the dis-eased area and dislodge the blocked energy that is causing the mental or emotional problems. There is no wasted time in long or unproductive discussions of the symptoms or the effects of problems prior to treatment of their cause. Our medicine immediately recognizes and dispels the sources of anguish and transforms those conditions into productive energy for the total good of the persons.

Our instruction in the natural sciences also differs greatly from yours. We have no theories or erroneous conclusions that lead only to misinformation or failure on the way to accurate understanding. We study the universal laws of natural sciences, God's laws. We apply them in structural ways here and assist in the ideas and conceptual learning phases of scientists on Earth.

As genetically gifted people, your scientists are both capable of absorbing information and receptive to that process. Specially selected scientists are privileged by a panel of our masters to absorb the information that is eternally available in the universal mind. It's an extraction and distillation process. Thus, the discoveries of Earth researchers and inventors are the scientific realities *that already exist in the universe*—they don't originate with your scientists. Our assistance is by way of what you could call the inspirations your scientists get, but what is really happening is that they're being responsive to the information being "fed" to them.

This same "feeding" principle applies to the arts. You are about equal with us in this area, because artistic expression comes from the universal melting pot of talent. This is a soul level connection that allows the universal gifts to flow freely, without the distortion inherent in the limitations of your third density bodies. Science is mental, art is from the heart and soul.

In painting and sculpture we are more discriminating in what we consider art and what you produce and prize. Some of your products are merely from audacious imaginations, and although the ideas remain as their own rigid forms, those types of products are not recognized as art and are not respected here. Your most beautiful soul expressions in painting and sculpture were generated in the heavens.

We have our own artists, of course. When the same geniuses known on Earth are here between embodiments, they instruct as well as produce new art forms. Their teaching and creative methods may not always be with brush and pigments or sculpting tools and marble, but some do enjoy that form and choose it over the mental and emotional manifestation process.

When those artistically endowed souls reincarnate, their new lifetimes are graced with soul level connection to universal beauty, but they may express that in different pathways. The sculptor last time may be a poet now, and the writer last time, a pianist. The teacher may emerge in the soul whose last lifetime was as a performing artist, or vice versa, but always the soul connection with the universal art is the key. It is the combination of that special connection and genetic inheritance that produces artistic genius. The soul chooses the parents for the genetic strain as well as the capability to provide instruction. They enter into a pre-birth agreement that includes a provision for an environment and the resources that will permit the artist to flourish and have access to all necessary training.

S: You keep amazing me! Do the "lazy souls" there waste their talents by not bringing them into their next physical lifetime?

MATTHEW: A talent may be wasted in a discarnate or incarnate lifetime, but this doesn't often happen. The urge to create is too strongly entrenched at soul level to be suppressed. That's why many masters in the arts overcome extreme obstacles to allow their creative drive to flow naturally—consider Beethoven! However, when an unforeseen situation prevents the pre-birth provisions from being realized, that talent is not lost. Its energy joins thought forms of like nature and will be attracted by other desirous souls for developing.

MUSIC

MATTHEW: Of all the arts, music is the most important here. I have spoken about our magnificent concerts, but music holds much greater significance for us than that— it's vital to our very existence! The perimeters of this realm are dependent upon the frequencies of music. The vibrations, especially from the strings, are part of what keeps the entire realm in attunement. Also, music is the single most effective medicine for the soul, and the energy of music is indispensable in our treatment of the traumatized psyches that come here. So, although respect and reverence are given to all masters, you can see why the highest honors are given to the most distinguished souls in music.

Unlike the personalized views from our windows or the weather we can create at will, music is all encompassing. It exists throughout the realm for all to tune into at the same frequency, so we can hear it whenever we wish by tuning into it on radio waves. You do the same with a radio, and you have radio stations with people who select the music to air. Here we serve as our own radio waves, stations and selectors.

S: Do you have real instruments and musicians, or is music its own energy form?

MATTHEW: That's an interesting concept, Mother, but our music is more down to Earth than that. We have many more stringed instruments and musicians than all your symphony orchestras combined, and a multitude of master harpists. That may be why the usual depiction of Heaven in paintings is full of angels with harps. None of our harpists are floating around on clouds, though!

S: Well, so much for that lovely idea! Is all of your music similar to our classical?

MATTHEW: That's backwards. Your music is more than similar to ours, it was complete in the heavens *prior* to being written on Earth. The composers may think of it as inspiration, but it is more accurately *filtration*. All the major themes, all the combinations of notes and chords, were here in that form prior to the composers absorbing it and filtering it through their minds—through their SOULS!—onto paper.

Not all of the musical beauty available for absorption has been captured in compositions anywhere, but some of the most magnificent tones in Creation already are on Earth. In centuries past there was considerable similarity in the majestic music taught and produced here and that absorbed by composers and musical artists on Earth. Sadly, in recent years less of the soul-universe musical connection is being registered there.

S: *Is the music that's "fed" to us meant to be for more than enjoyment—maybe an emotional catharsis?*

MATTHEW: YES! That's exactly why this music of the heavenly spheres is available throughout the universe! Music is continuously being created here for all of our own needs, and it's being transmitted and absorbed continuously into Earth mentality to allow suppressed feelings there to be felt and released. Releasing and positively transmuting that kinetic energy heals the soul, and the ripple effect benefits the entire universe.

But definitely not all music popular on Earth has its source here! Divine music has no cacophonous sounds, unlike the heavy metal and hard rock and even some jazz and neoclassical compositions prevalent there. Those raucous types of compositions may allow a great deal of angry, rebellious energy to be expressed in the writing, playing and listening, but the negatively charged energy being produced by those sounds is not being transmuted, it's swirling right there around you.

Loud discordant music—NOISE!—agitates the spirit and creates imbalance within the human psyche. As the imbalance increases, the psyche's capacity to absorb light energy decreases. Consistent decreasing eventually can destroy that capacity altogether. Generating imbalance is one of the dark forces' most effective strategies on Earth, and the kind of music that accomplishes it is one of their tools. Thus, without the awareness of the composers, musicians and listeners, they are being drawn into darkness. The sound they think captivates them actually is *capturing* them, because it is strategically designed by the darkness to stunt spiritual growth and adversely affect emotional, physical and mental integrity.

EMOTIONS

S: Good morning, Matthew!

MATTHEW: Good morning yourself, Mother. It's wonderful to feel you smiling so much today.

S: You can feel *me smiling?*

MATTHEW: Not exactly, I just simplified my thought. I feel the same happiness that's been causing you to smile so much this morning. Remember, we feel the emotions of people with whom we're bonded. Fortunately there's a protective layer that shields us from feeling all the emotions collectively affecting people there. Believe me, this would never be considered Heaven without that shield!

We feel that we're in the most loving and satisfying of all placements at this stage of our soul evolution. Still, we do feel a great deal that isn't attributed to a blissful, peaceful, harmonious Heaven. Those wonderful sensations are pervasive here, but we also experience emotions that could be called reflective, serious, sobering and even downright negative.

On Earth it seems as if the horrors in a country half a world away are relatively unfelt by those who don't personally suffer them. More in a mental than an emotional state do you consider those distant people who live in anguish and fear and extreme deprivation. Our work with souls transitioning from those circumstances is carried on in the midst of their intense feelings. The negativity of their sorrow, fright, physical pain and anger arrives here en masse continuously. The entire realm is affected, not only those of us whose direct service so closely touches those emotions.

Most of us are not far from physical experiencing, you know. We can relate to the ordeals these newly arrived souls have so recently endured and we can empathize with their feelings. It's a separate issue from our ongoing karmic lessons and spiritual growth. It is actually feeling the very same emotions as the people do who arrive in great pain in body, mind and spirit.

Furthermore, since the essence of our being allows for intensified sensations, the emotions we feel are heightened beyond those felt on the Earth plane. The density of your bodies dulls positive emotions and traps negative emotions. When negative emotions are trapped for a while, dis-ease occurs. Even though you have myriad diagnoses, trapped energy is the root cause of all your illnesses. The same spectrum of diagnoses is given as reasons for physical death, and that is not correct, either. The cessation of energy contraction and expansion on a rhythmic basis is the reason the physical body dies.

I digressed, Mother, but I thought you would be interested in knowing that. Now then, the other side of our intensified sensations is that positive feelings are pure joy to experience! This gives balance to the painful sensations we share with the arrivals. It could not be otherwise in this realm because balance is necessary for soul growth. Love here is purer than on Earth, and it is without any of your volatile sensations of "falling in love" or out of it. Our enjoyment of music or any scene or activity is more intense and purer than yours, also.

S: Do you feel any emotions that we don't?

MATTHEW: What an interesting question, Mother! No, I don't think so. The major difference is in the purity of our emotions. We feel only our primary emotion about any situation.

S: What do you mean by "primary" emotion?

MATTHEW: I'll give you an example. You feel genuinely happy for your dearest friend, who, after a long, desperate time of unemployment and anxiety, just succeeded in getting a good job at the large company where you're working. But your happiness for her may not be free of undercurrent emotions. Perhaps you doubt that she is capable of performing her new responsibilities well enough to keep the job, and worry how losing it would affect her. Perhaps you feel envy because she got exactly the type of job she wanted and you had settled for one that doesn't really satisfy you. Maybe you're relieved that she got the job because she left the running for another position that you also had applied for. Or maybe you're jealous because she got the very job you wanted to switch to but weren't chosen to fill. Or, if you hadn't known about that job vacancy, you may feel regret that you didn't have the opportunity to apply. Maybe you feel resentment or anger that your qualifications were known to exactly fit the job description, but the vacancy was advertised instead of being offered to you.

So you see the wide variety of possible companion feelings that may be fleeting or may last along with your primary one of happiness for your dearest friend. In short, rarely do you separate your feelings about another person or any situation from your perception of how you yourself are, or may be, affected. That doesn't happen here.

S: That is thought provoking, Matthew. How do souls there overcome those negative companion feelings? And what about bullies, snobs, trouble-making gossipers, braggarts and other rather obnoxious but not "evil" types?

MATTHEW: Undesirable characteristics do accompany people to this realm, but those traits don't remain long. Here we acknowledge our character and personality shortcomings, whereas all too often people on Earth recognize them only in others.

When the cumulative soul examines its lifeprint in the Akashic Records, reviewing the immediate past life and evaluating it in conjunction with all prior lifetimes is a great lesson in itself. When a review shows that undesirable traits have been pointed out repeatedly without improvement in lifetime after lifetime, the soul can make intense efforts while here—often with counseling—to overcome that pattern.

S: But in the meantime, who would want to have them around? That doesn't seem to fit into the rest of Heaven.

MATTHEW: Well, Mother, they *wouldn't* be around anyone who doesn't want them! An energy is attached to every human characteristic. Like all else in existence, personality traits come within the universal law of like attracts like. Each trait is channeled into sections of "like" aspects, so souls with undesirable traits simply aren't around "unlike" souls who don't attract that energy. However, if a soul's lesson selection during this spirit life includes tolerance or patience, they may require proximity with characteristics they formerly couldn't tolerate.

S: You know, Matthew, there seems to be constant emphasis there on learning and growing, and even with all the recreation you have, life sounds basically so focused and serious. Don't you people ever laugh?

MATTHEW: You can bet we do! The principle of like attracts like applies in this laughing matter as in all other energy attachments, so here just as there, laughter is infectious and its influence has a wonderful ripple effect. Like all other traits that make transition with people, the ability to laugh heartily or to create good humor also arrives continuously. Of course, it doesn't emerge quickly in souls with damaged physical bodies or traumatized psyches, but with recuperation, that aspect of their personalities starts coming forth. After a certain point of recovery, good humor and amusing situations around them aid in their progress. When they start laughing, we know it's a leap forward in their restoration to sound health. We're glad that your medical profession has discovered this ancient truth.

Often we see a perverse sense of humor on Earth, so a laughable situation here may be different from your own, but not in all ways, of course. You've always appreciated dry humor and quick wit, Mother. They're here in abundance because our subjects for humor are refined. We have marvelous theatrical comedy productions and also performances by masterful comedians. Your greatest comic entertainers eventually perform here, too, you know—the ultimate in taking their show on the road, you might say.

Mother, surely you couldn't think this would be Heaven without good humor and laughter!

EMPLOYMENT

S: Do you have jobs that correspond to ours?

MATTHEW: There are differences in our system and yours, but similarities as well, and everyone who wishes to work has a variety of opportunities.

With music's vital importance to this realm, it's natural that many are involved in that field. In addition to those who are using music therapy for the healing of newly arrived souls who need it, a great number are working in the entertainment area. This includes musicians, singers, stagehands for the concerts, instrument manifesters, and all those who are composing, teaching, and learning different phases of music-making. Sometimes music employs the largest number of workers. At other times more people are in the soul transition assistance field, the welcomers and medical assisters. This is the field I'm in. It is the most fluctuating of all in worker numbers because it's directly related to happenings on Earth. Right now the many civil wars, disease epidemics, starvation and weather-related disasters that are causing mass death on Earth are making transition assistance the largest in work activity. Of all our employment areas, transition assistance and music always are first or second in prominence.

Education is a major field, as you can imagine from our strong emphasis on learning. Not only teaching, but also all the services and activities related to the academic world come under this heading. Because learning is the principal endeavor of so many souls, being a student is considered employment, too. Just like there, we study for advanced degrees in preparation for higher-level teaching or other professional responsibilities. Often we take subjects meant only for personal interest and enjoyment and then find that they become applicable to our work.

Administration is a big and important area. Just like on Earth, this is the clerical, detailed end of keeping things running smoothly and efficiently, but we have considerable differences. Here this field also includes management and the handling of all the settlement needs of arrivals, and there's no paperwork. We don't have a bureaucracy, but there is a defined structure of responsibility allocations and a system of operations, otherwise this realm wouldn't have the orderliness that prevails.

In our standing management the Council is the highest. The members not only cover order and structure here, they interface with the governing bodies of those realms with which we interact. In the case of Earth, interaction isn't with your government officials, but with the angelic and spirit realm representatives and other extraterrestrial entities operating on the planet in myriad capacities during this time of great commotion and change.

Construction is a major employment area. We've talked about manifestation, the means whereby our buildings are erected, and many souls are employed in these various design and construction processes. Workers in this field also maintain all public and neighborhood buildings, and landscaping comes under this category, too.

Entertainment other than music provides work for a large number of us—writers, actors, stage crews, scenery and costume designers and manifesters, technicians—all the jobs to put on a grand production there, just no ushers needed.

We've also talked about the care of our babies and youngsters. The caretakers are carefully selected individuals with unique aptitude for nurturing, and their service is immensely gratifying to them and honored by all. While fewer in numbers than in those larger fields I've mentioned, the people in this service are vitally important to us.

Those are our primary employment areas, Mother, but all work here is cherished because it is helping others in one way or another. As one grows in knowledge and experience, he is given correspondingly greater responsibility in progressively higher realms of work and spiritual evolvement.

S: Matthew, those kinds of work require talents, skills or education that most of the world's population don't have. What do all of those unprepared people do when they get there? And what about people who labored hard all their lives here and might prefer not to work there?

MATTHEW: Mother, you're forgetting that it is the *cumulative* soul who is here, not only the personage who has made transition. Much more experience and knowledge is within each soul than you're thinking! It is true that a soul who has had very few physical lifetimes would not have the skills and aptitudes of souls who have experienced many embodiments, but appropriate training is available to all at their level of interest and ability.

We have other greatly different working circumstances from yours, too. Since there's no need to be employed from a salary standpoint, a job is not a necessity, it is only a pleasurable growth experience. There are no work assignments, only choices of occupation, and we can easily change jobs whenever we want. If someone wants to work in a different field from those he knows, he may enter any one that appeals to him, regardless of how specialized it may be, because there's access to whatever training or studies might be needed. Since brain function here is greater than on Earth due to our lighter density, learning comes more easily and swiftly, so preparation for a new field of endeavor is not a formidable prospect.

Another way employment here differs from yours is attitude and expectations. There are no controlling or intimidating boss-employee relationships, no ruthless competition for jobs, no anxiety about job loss in a merger, no quotas to fill, no comparison with anyone else's activity or productivity, no mind-numbing monotonous jobs, no vying for promotions, no deadlines, and no pressure to succeed. In short, we avoid those negative work aspects you deal with on Earth.

All of us can find any number of ways to live a satisfying and productive life, with or without regular employment. Some lives are less work-oriented than others, but they can be just as purposeful and fulfilling. Some souls may spend their lives here resting and healing and growing through expanded awareness. Others may choose to combine "retirement" with what you call volunteer work, or tutor in a specialized area where they have expertise, or pursue old or new hobbies. True relaxation is at such a premium on Earth that most people don't have that luxury which is so necessary for restoration of a weary spirit.

TRANSITIONING SOULS

S: Matthew, what do you do as a medical assister?

MATTHEW: I've been wondering when you would ask that, Mother! You ask Eric about the progress of his company and ask Betsy about her teaching and ask Michael how his sales are coming along. And you've asked me about those important aspects of their lives, but until now, you've never asked me about MY work!

I know that in the past mediums have told you what I'm doing, but this is the *first time* you have thought of me in the same natural way you do your other children, by directly talking *with me* about what I'm doing. Mother, do you see the great difference in how we in this realm are regarded versus people on Earth? *Even by you!*

S: . . . You're right, Matthew. I don't know what else to say.

MATTHEW: I can feel your heavy distress, Mother, and I didn't mean to cause that. I overreacted to your question, and I'm sorry. This has given me new insight and a valuable reminder that some things I still expect. Having expectations of others is just as undesirable as making a judgment, which I also was doing. Now I see my need to more readily recognize and avoid these two characteristics, as progress in spiritual growth, here or there, is outgrowing them. You see, just as I've told you several other times, you still are giving me opportunities to learn from you!

I'm glad you're feeling better about this, Mother. So am I. Now then, I'm immensely pleased to tell you what I do! In brief, I help souls who need specialized assistance after their arrival. Like the others in the soul transition assistance field, I think of my work as a service, not as a job.

I didn't start as a medical assister. After I adjusted to leaving my Earth lifetime, I became a welcomer, which is greeting transitioning souls who arrive in relatively healthy psychic condition. At that same time I was studying medicine and, later, psychology. Then, in addition to my greeting work, I started helping babies and little children adjust to this realm. That experience and my studies led to my initial assignment as medical assister.

When I became proficient at helping the souls whose situations were especially difficult, I was assigned permanently to this specialized assistance. I moved along the ranks quite rapidly to a position of higher responsibility than most of the others. That meant a greater number of assisters to be responsible for as well as personally tending the most difficult arrivals' particular needs.

Without scanning for an accurate count, I'd say that I have treated about 10,000 people. That's not counting the ones I helped as a greeter or those who didn't require much medical attention, but only the more difficult souls whom I helped to make transition. Maybe that doesn't seem like a lot for the time I've been here, but most of those souls required intensive and lengthy therapy, and, just as physicians there remain with their patients until full health is restored, I do also.

Mother, the reception and care of arrivals is so crucial for people on Earth to know that I want to explain the entire process starting at the beginning, with what you call death and we call transition. When the physical body dies, there is an instantaneous adjustment in the electrical system of the etheric body so it can leave Earth intact and arrive in Nirvana already attuned to the higher frequency here. That adjustment is made in the lightning flash moment when the etheric body separates from the physical body and clothes the soul for its alignment on the way to that light passage often described as a tunnel in the "near-death experience."

There is absolutely NOTHING stressful or fearful about that journey! But it happens so quickly that the arrival's memories of circumstances *immediately prior* to transition are as real upon entry here as they were when the person was experiencing those circumstances on Earth. The memories profoundly affect the arrival's capacity to adjust to his etheric body, and when the memories are of traumatic experiences, a personalized and usually long healing process is required.

Since the etheric body has been with the soul throughout its physical lifetime, it is intact when it enters with the soul into this realm, but it needs assistance to usher in its strength. When the arrival is in sound condition, that ushering-in process can be accomplished with ease. In the case of a severely traumatized arrival, the process requires the combined energy of a highly trained medical assister and an attendant group of ten aides.

It is the unique soul energy stream of each arrival that lets us know his identity and psychic condition. Through an energy correlation process, each arrival enters the station appropriate for his immediate needs. The energy streams also let us anticipate the number of arrivals so that sufficient assistance always is at the ready.

Although telepathic communication can be understood by arrivals, native speech is important, particularly in a stressful entry, so the welcomers and assisters converse with them in their native tongues. Many of us study languages in order to do this.

The welcomers, who also may be called transition greeters, are the first to meet arrivals at our "regular" entry stations. They're like hospitality people anywhere who assist newcomers, and they're present in addition to family and friends on hand. Often emotionally well-adjusted arrivals need only greeting and introduction to the realm. In this case, the welcomers describe the spectrum of the realm's accommodations for their immediate needs, comfort and interests. Housing, food, studies, employment, social events, the realm's governing system—all of that is explained prior to the administrators becoming involved in the actual logistics of helping the arrivals get settled.

Mother, you've been thinking how impersonal it is to refer to the arriving souls as "arrivals." Yes, it is, and I'm doing this only so you can distinguish between *persons* in arrival status and their own souls, as well as to differentiate between those newly arrived souls and the soul population already here. As you're thinking, "newcomers" sounds a lot friendlier, but there are constantly newcomers to the realm who are not transitioning from Earth. Our general word for arrivals is "souls," but every one of them is known by name and addressed by name. So you see, our reception of every "arrival" *is* intensely personal, and all care is individualized for the specific needs of each.

S: Thank you for mentioning that. Let me get in a question here. You've said that we remember our other lifetimes when we enter Nirvana, so why is the same information given about the realm every time?

MATTHEW: Memories of other lifetimes don't come instantly at the soul's moment of entry. When there is an easy and quick adjustment, full awareness of previous residency here emerges smoothly and steadily, like molasses being poured, not like toast popping up. Remembering comes more slowly to arrivals who need "regular" medical assistance and much more slowly to those whose death was under traumatic circumstances.

Re-introduction, if you will, to the realm is gracious, considerate and helpful, and I assure you, it is welcomed by the arrivals.

Now then, people who need "regular" medical assistance are those whose experiences immediately prior to transition were relatively free of trauma, but due to debilitated health, their physical bodies have a lingering hold over the etheric bodies. We must treat that condition so the etheric bodies are not injured. These arrivals enter at treatment stations with tranquil, quietly cheerful private rooms and wards, where sweet-smelling natural fragrances lightly fill the air and pastel colors waft like fluttering sheer curtains at an open window. Outdoors in these areas the sky is softly blue, not its usual brilliance, and there are warm, light breezes. Soothing music is almost inaudible, yet gently stirring for the emotions due to its beautiful chords and fragile harp-like sounds. The entire setting is fluid, with a sensation of soft, warm motion, and all elements are gentle in composition, color and tone.

This restorative setting is ideal for arrivals with relatively healthy psyches and bodies that endured only a short terminal illness, or bodies frail and weary simply from a very long time of functioning. Even though these arrivals don't require any extreme measures of medical care during their recuperation, always medical assisters are in attendance because this is reassuring to the convalescents.

The reception and treatment environment is much different for arrivals in acute distress. They enter at intensive care stations where they immediately start receiving individualized care. In treating these traumatized arrivals we are dealing with both the body and the damaged psyche. Whereas the soul is liberated into spiritual awareness, the person's psyche is still operating at its lowered capacity in the last events experienced by the physical body on Earth. The soul is *constant*. It grows from the experiences, but it is beyond the captive aspect of the psyche, which has great need for healing. Without the healing, life here, just as anywhere else, would be hell for those people with brutalized psyches.

Some of them endured lengthy illness that caused intense physical pain, vastly restricted activity, and grief. Perhaps fear, also, and sorrowful regret at their conditions' effects on family and friends. The etheric bodies of those souls who are worn out from battling disease, debilitation and anxiety have to be medically tended because the memory of physical pain is powerful even in the shadow effects associated with loss, mutilation or degeneration of physical body parts. Obviously, these people's spirits also are in need of tender nurturing for recuperation, so both medical and psychological care is required.

The same is true of arrivals whose physical death was caused quickly by massive injuries, perhaps in vehicle crashes or fires or violent storms or earthquakes. The psyches of people who were tortured and murdered suffer profound trauma, as do war victims—troops maimed and killed in combat as well as the civilian innocents whose Earth lives were ended by the horrors of war. People who made transition during or soon after any of these situations arrive traumatized in spirit beyond description, still psychically experiencing their recent terror on Earth.

Rarely do they understand that they now are safe in this realm. They believe they have been rescued from the hell so recently endured, but usually they think the rescue was on Earth. When they no longer need the ultimate in private care, they are moved to rehabilitation wards where their recovery is aided by therapists in an atmosphere carefully designed to uplift their spirits and give reassurance of their healing progress.

There is another kind of arrival very needful of loving attendance. Those who come with heavy guilt, remorse or sorrow require extensive psychological care to heal their damaged psyches. Generally they respond more quickly than the arrivals from traumatic physical deaths, but not always. When those emotional conditions are in conjunction with other psychic and physical traumas, recovery and adjustment time is far greater.

S: With realigning energy and providing a healing musical environment as your only treatment modalities, I don't understand where all the individualized care comes in.

MATTHEW: This isn't a cookie-cutter Heaven, Mother. We reach out to each soul in its most recent incarnated personage, and personalized care and conversation is just as essential here as it is for all patients in hospitals on Earth. It's exactly those same psyches we greet and assist in adjustment here. We have the advantage that the soul remembrance comes forth as soon as people adjust to being here, but as I have told you, it comes much more slowly to those who arrive in seriously traumatized condition.

S: Is there group treatment, like our support groups for people who have suffered similar devastation?

MATTHEW: No. Every arrival's treatment is customized throughout recovery. Not even families are treated in a group when they make transition simultaneously or within moments of each other. Each soul arrives by itself and is treated individually because each has unique needs requiring instant and intimate attention. Those who were together at the time of death may wish to be reunited, and that happens as soon as they are healed enough to do so.

S: I think it would be beneficial healing-wise and compassionate to treat family members who died at the same time or within moments of each other as a group so they can know they're all together.

MATTHEW: Mother, I'll give you an example of why that can't be done. A mother is in pain from injuries in a civil war she abhors, in shock and grief for her little daughter who has just died in her arms after a brief illness, and in great anxiety because her teenaged son is in the thick of combat. Moments later she arrives here, after a fatal head injury from flying debris, and her anguish, fear and pain are as acute as they were during the area-wide bombing that caused her physical death.

Her son is in excellent health until the moment he is blown to bits in that same bombing that caused his mother's death. He has no knowledge of what has happened to his mother and sister. He is young, imbued with a sense of indestructibility that tempers his fear in battle. Furthermore, he was schooled in war and taught to consider it his right and responsibility to kill the "enemy." You can see that both his psyche and his body would require considerably different treatment than either his mother or his sister needs. That is why group treatment, even for a small family, never would be attempted. It would not even be possible, because it is the *individual* soul, not unified souls, that makes transition.

S: Thank you for explaining that, Matthew. All of this is so new to me that I guess I'm superimposing on Nirvana what could happen in the same situations here.

MATTHEW: Mother, it's natural that you would try to relate to some of the things I tell you, because other things are so astounding to you that sometimes you think I don't know what I'm talking about.

Now then, I'll give you an actual example of how we treat a traumatized arrival. You are seeing a wounded soldier in combat uniform sitting on a cot, in heat-of-battle anger, fear and fighting forcefulness, and someone who is gently trying to soothe him. Just as in the image I'm sending, the soldier's body appears here to be solid, like Earth flesh, and the cot also appears to be solid. That is an illusion we manifest because it is necessary at this stage of his acclimation to this realm.

Soldiers in combat have to balance the reality of death with a sense of their own invincibility so they can focus on survival. This difficult psychic maneuvering, plus the shock of battle and the horror of being surrounded by dead comrades and the screams of the wounded, has put this soldier in an extremely agitated state. It's necessary to let him realize that this is a change from his last Earth surroundings, which we do by easing the battlefield conditions in which he had been living and dying. Little by little his last memories are eliminated by that gradual removal of the scene around him until he is able to accept that he has left his Earth body and has entered this new life. The transition must be slow and realistic to him or his psyche will be shocked into a state where healing is a major repair. Not that the assistance already needed and being rendered isn't of major significance, but I am speaking relatively.

S: It would seem that realism for that soldier would mean having acres of fighting around him. Can he see his dead comrades if they're receiving the same kind of treatment nearby? Well, since you've said every soul arrives separately, I suppose he's alone with his medical attendant in a battlefield atmosphere.

MATTHEW: No, Mother, he's not the only soldier there—I just sent you a close-up image so you could clearly see the solidity of his body and the cot. Yes, he can see some of his "dead" comrades nearby, and that is at once helpful and a hindrance because of possible confusion, as other men he just as recently had seen are not there. Grouping these men at this stage is not in conflict with our treating each arrival individually in accordance with specific healing needs. To avoid further psychic damage, it is essential that these soldiers' dying environment be portrayed accurately, and their comrades' presence is part of this realism.

This group of soldiers who were killed almost simultaneously numbers about ten, with varying attitudes regarding death and Heaven. They arrived at stations where their soul level energy permitted and their psychic adjustment can best be served, the initial stage of which you just were viewing. Each in the group has his own energy attunement to follow from this point forward. Some of these men may be quite advanced in soul evolution and very soon be aware of their entry into the spirit realm. We have seen newly arrived soldiers with such advanced evolvement that they knew instantly where they were and quickly helped others nearby accept their transition. Other men in this group may have very serious review ahead.

As for the image you saw, yes, it was only a small portion of a reenacted battle environment, minus the deafening sounds and the gore of Earth reality. However, "acres of battle" would not have been an accurate image to send you because we don't see that, either. What we see is more like flash scenes in a movie, where viewers have a glimpse of one character and his situation, then another character and his, and so on. Even though a little time is spent developing each vignette, viewers are meant to understand that all of the developments are happening simultaneously.

We see glimpses of individual souls in varying stages of comprehension and needs for transition assistance. We're led to the place where we need to be by the energy connection that is established. I know you're wondering how the differentiation can be achieved in that chaos, and I don't know how to explain this to you, Mother, but I can assure you that it works to perfection.

As I've mentioned before, our primary healing mechanism is vibrations, which is why music is so essential. Healthy individuals here have a vibratory rate between two definite points, allowing for some variation corresponding to rising or falling enthusiasm, excitement, or whatever emotion causes a rate change. Since we have no fearful or angering circumstances to deal with, a rise from the normal rate is only for positive reasons. Arrivals have a much different set of rates, which are geared to their belief systems throughout life on Earth and the circumstances of physical life and death.

S: I see. Are children received the same as adults?

MATTHEW: Every child is greeted with special tenderness and loving energy and given the same personal and diligent care as all other souls. Children who arrive in comparatively sound body and mind soon are able to join the children in the large cheerful homes I've described, where they are lovingly nurtured.

Children with acute needs for physical or psychic healing receive continuous customized care and medical expertise in an environment designed appropriately for their age and condition, with some appointments manifested to be happily familiar to the child. With progress toward health, the child is treated to companions other than the constant caregivers and entertainment suitable for his or her recovery level.

Understandably, the younger the children are when they come, the easier they adjust to the realm. Older children remember more and are more aware of missing Earth family for the time their souls are growing beyond their psyches.

Once that happens—and again, in some cases this is almost immediate because of soul evolvement—they eagerly join the other children in those inviting big homes and enthusiastically embark upon a happy fulfilling life.

S: If their families could know this, it could be such a great comfort to them. I have more questions. How many transition assisters are there in total, and how many are on duty at any one time? Do you have scheduled work periods and time off? Without clocks or any sense of our time, how do you know when to report and leave?

MATTHEW: I can't give you an exact total, Mother, but millions are trained in this field. That "count" doesn't include welcomers, only medical assisters. With souls constantly leaving as well as arriving, and naturally, the departures include many in our field, I'd say that only our census takers know moment by moment exact numbers of us with sufficient training to fill service posts. As is true on Earth, there are ascending degrees of expertise and experience, with corresponding degrees of responsibilities. Interns, you might call them, are not given full-time assignments until they have mastered all of the education and training and completed a period of supervised service, and until then they are not considered part of our ranks. Also, please remember that each assister stays with the souls he met at transition until their recovery is complete, and many of us cannot add to our "case load."

The number of assisters on duty varies with the situations on Earth, but always enough of us are on hand so that arrivals never are left ungreeted instantly or unattended in any moment. With deaths happening there en masse, many thousands of us are ready to meet and assist in the first instant of transition. There aren't thousands of separate entrances, but there are thousands of individual entries, often simultaneously, say casualties of a massive earthquake who are in addition to those who are dying from all other causes. Space is not a consideration since we don't have the bulk of physical bodies needing room as you perceive it.

No reason is urgent enough for any assister—or welcomer—to desert the service post and leave arrivals unattended. Since time doesn't exist, it's not easy to assess how long we work without a break, and since we have no sensation of tiring physically or emotionally, fatigue is not a limiting factor. We simply work as needed. When many arrivals are anticipated, obviously more assisters are needed and for longer periods.

We have an infallible energy notification system. A series of energy pulses lets us know whether the worker ranks are filled or are in need of replacements or additions. Because of our great numbers, not all of us are needed at once even in those peak times in numbers of arrivals, but it isn't a haphazard arrangement of simply whoever feels like it can show up, such as when relatives or friends may be arriving.

When the need is automatically registered through the energy connections, at only a thought we are transported to the scene. When another soul already is there, the second to arrive may stay for a team effort or move to the next energy blip that signals another imminent arrival.

S: How do you arrange free time for our sittings and all your other interests and activities?

MATTHEW: We have an established hierarchy responsible for the overall welcoming and assisting of arrivals, and when all service posts are manned, the rest of us are free to be doing whatever we wish. That is true for all souls here—we never feel work interferes with our other avenues of interest. My work is not only a significant accomplishment, it is a great pleasure and honor to be involved in this service at my level of responsibility. And I can assure you, Mother, I have plenty of time for all of my other pursuits!

S: What happens if you are on duty and you learn that one of your family here has an emergency?

MATTHEW: If I were attending an arrival and you were in an emergency situation, this is how things would proceed. Gregory, your guardian angel, would be the first contact with your emergency vibration. His energy call automatically would reach me and all others in this realm who are closely bonded with you. When I receive this notification I summon my assistant, who is trained to take over. He instantly appears on the scene. Then I'm released of the

energy bond with the arrival and I can direct this energy
toward bonding with you. All of this happens within a wink,
like a light coming on, yet many steps of energy bonding
and releasing are accomplished so there is no delay in reaching you and no interruption in aid to the arrival.

*S: Matthew, thank you for all of this information. I never
imagined that such complex care and coordination would be
needed—and supplied—there.*

MATTHEW: There's another aspect of all this that I
think you'll find interesting, Mother. When each person
arrives, Nirvana is exactly what that individual imagined
Heaven to be during his Earth lifetime. The energy of the
convictions within the individual's psyche creates for him
the Heaven of those convictions. Usually this is in great error!

The truth of Nirvana comes to each person with adjustment to being here. Maybe I should say that accepting
that truth *is* the adjustment. It is not what the person's
soul realizes, but what the person's *psyche* holds. During
the period of remembering what this realm truly is—because
the knowledge IS there, it simply has been forgotten—the
arrival's erroneous ideas remain intact psychically, but they
cannot be permitted to remain very long.

Every soul's realities affect this placement, but the
effects are especially impactive when those realities differ
from the universal laws. The energy frequency of all souls
in this level of the realm is the same, otherwise they
couldn't even enter here. But their thought forms in error
of the truth and their negative attitudes in any respect
cannot be allowed to continue because they would change
our entire energy field.

That is one reason the therapy so carefully designed
for each individual is of paramount importance. Our entry

stations are far more than gracious welcome areas and medical care facilities. They are the initial stage of adroit efforts to quickly transmute that negatively-affected energy that is so pervasive in arrivals and avert its proliferation.

S: It's almost overwhelming to think about all of this, Matthew, but it's comforting, too. Heaven definitely is NOT just the eternal serenity and all-knowing place I used to think it is! On a lighter note, what do you wear when you're working?

MATTHEW: We wear whatever is expected by each arrival, and because we are completely aware of all the expectations of each, we know ahead of time the most appropriate dress. A familiar Earth-type outfit helps prevent further shock to people who need easing into this placement, so we wear whatever is in keeping with the circumstances of the people's physical death.

For instance, at the hospital stations for arrivals from Western cultures, the usual clothing is the white or pastel-colored uniform of your medical professions, or casual clothing, most often jeans and T-shirts. When arrivals come from cold climates, they most recently have seen people in heavy coats, so we wear heavy coats. Attire familiar to soldiers would be a uniform like their medics wear, while a member of a street gang would more likely expect to see someone in sneakers, jeans and leather jackets, and we dress accordingly.

Jeans, the universal dress code on Earth, is much more common wear for our welcomers and medical assisters than white robes. However, arrivals who pass over due to long-term illness, or simply many decades of living, usually are met by welcomers in white robes, or perhaps suits or dresses. People in fragile conditions are expecting to die, you could say, and they feel more comfortable seeing someone in a traditional white outfit they've associated with the pearly gates.

For arrivals from areas where ethnic dress is common, we wear outfits appropriate to their regions, and for tribal populations, the ceremonial attire of the gods of their religions. It takes no extra effort to be thoughtful in this respect. It's just as easy for us to manifest a lavish headdress or multicolored gown as it is white robes and jeans.

S: That is such a sensitive and practical consideration. I never thought before what you'd be wearing when I arrive— now I'll expect to see you in jeans. What do Nirvana's residents typically wear?

MATTHEW: During adjustment to the realm they usually wear clothing they were accustomed to on Earth, so a wide variety of styles is always evident, but eventually a white robe with a sash becomes the usual choice for ordinary occasions. Because it's *comfortable,* Mother, that's why!

SUICIDE

S: Are people who die by suicide treated differently from the others?

MATTHEW: Yes and no. They are given the same personal, loving reception as all other arrivals, and every effort is extended to assist in their healing and adjustment just as it is with all other traumatized souls who need customized treatment. However, they enter at a special treatment station because their traumas need a unique kind of maximum care.

I know you have heard that people who take their own lives face a punishing form of spirit life, but instinctively you doubt this is so. You are right, it is not so. It isn't fair or reasonable to lump all suicides into one category with one exacting judgment for all to face up to. In some cases the cause of suicide is severe body chemistry imbalance that impairs sound decision-making. In other cases, what you call insanity leads to suicide. Some people act out of extreme depression, perhaps due to loss of someone they considered vital to their lives, and depression takes over their rational thinking. Some take their lives on foolish dares, not believing the risk would result in death. Others act in despair of the moment rather than give the spirit time to be strengthened. Some end their lives to end intractable pain. None of those is more reason for harsh judgment than death attributed to heart failure or a broken neck.

Some people in relatively sounder condition consciously decide to end their lives. For some, this is in total capitulation to a series of adverse events, sometimes to provide for their families in the only way they feel is left to them, insurance money. Other people conclude that they cannot deal with situations they find too difficult or unsavory— perhaps their marital infidelity or financial or political corruption has been discovered, or they have been discredited by their peers. These calculated cases also are very sad because those people really don't wish to leave the whole of their Earth life, only those aspects they see as so overwhelming that in their opinion, death is the only remedy.

Whatever their reason, people who commit suicide review their Akashic records with the same self-assessment and next lifetime planning process as any other soul. It is true that they incur an accumulated lesson by having to repeat all the lessons they chose but didn't complete, but there is no punishment or heavy karma levied due to self-inflicted death. *Intent,* or *motive,* is the basis for all determinations of self-judgment, and those people need not judge themselves any more severely than any others in this realm.

ADJUSTMENT TO THE REALM

S: How long does it take for people to adjust to being in Nirvana?

MATTHEW: Considering the difficulties of our establishing accurate time spans within your measurements, I think the best way to answer that is by categorizing arrivals whose living and dying circumstances were relatively free of trauma.

Some are so well prepared by their level of soul evolvement and completed Earth affairs that they need no transition assistance at all. These souls are welcomed by a cheering crowd when it is known they will be joining us. We wish there were many more of these!

The second category of arrivals could be classified as willing, but not completely ready to be here. Usually they lived only momentarily or a short time with their terminal condition, so their bodies are not stressed by long-term pain or wasted by disease and aging organ failure. These people are hesitant to accept the fact of transition because Earth life offered loving, pleasant relationships they cherish, and sometimes their work was so satisfying that they wish it also could continue. But they aren't as emotional as you might expect. Their emotions are balanced. They are half-reluctant to give up Earth life and half-welcoming the spirit realm once again—they are aware that they have *returned*. Their beliefs are not opposed to what they're encountering, so they are well adjusted in that regard. After pleasant discussions, both telepathic and in their Earth language, they accept their return to Nirvana quite rapidly.

Third in order of adjustment are the people who have been indoctrinated within strict church teachings. No religious dogma is the true, complete Christed messengers' accounts of Heaven or eternal life. The more incorrect the teachings and the longer the exposure to them, the more difficult it is to convince their adherents, Yes, this IS Heaven in that they no longer are living in their Earth bodies, and No, Heaven is NOT what they were taught. We can't let their initially permitted mistaken concepts of this realm continue very long because of those adverse effects that I spoke of, so Nirvana as it really is eventually must be shown to these folks. Their adjustment takes considerably longer than the previous two groups.

The last to accept this realm are people of stubborn nature whose rigid religious or scientific indoctrination opposes almost everything they encounter here. Rather than accept what is revealed to them, some put themselves into a netherland of discarnate souls—you could say ghosts—in an attempt to get back to their Earth lives. Some choose to sleep for a while, feeling certain that when they waken they will be either in their own beds at home or in the everlasting life of their concept. The most severe cases among these may sleep and waken intermittently for hundreds of years before recognizing that they simply had been incorrctly taught.

Again, the people in those four groupings came here in relatively healthy psychic condition, relatively free of trauma. There is no way to group in an adjustment time sense the souls who arrive with traumatized psyches and bodies, because their Earth lifetime experiences and physical death circumstances so profoundly affect their recovery period. They must heal completely before confronting whatever other adjustment they may require. As an aid to their healing, Nirvana is presented in accordance with their expectations until they have fully recovered. This is possible because their concepts in error of the truth are not their energy focus, their return to health is, and so no serious negativity results.

S: Does anything there fit into the purgatory concept?

MATTHEW: I surely would say so! Those people who—despite all that's revealed to them—refuse to even consider that this is the place where ALL Earth residents come after Earth life ends, who choose to sleep sometimes for centuries rather than even consider that their beliefs were simply based in false instruction—I think that's as close to purgatory as you can get!

I should add a word about the great benefit to this realm when new arrivals quickly adjust and take advantage of the wondrous and boundless growth opportunities here. The tiniest change here affects countless souls! This is true on Earth as well, but to a lesser degree. The energy motion is the same, as energy neither increases nor decreases in intensity without a soul's direction. However, on Earth the intent registered energetically is less intensely committed than the same here. The goodness in any person's incarnate character automatically grows in intensity when that soul comes to this realm.

NEAR-DEATH EXPERIENCE

S: I've heard from Betsy and a medium that you read Life After Life, *a book about near-death experiences. Have you ever seen anyone in that situation?*

MATTHEW: Yes, I read that book the last summer I was with you, and yes, I have seen many visiting souls who had been declared "clinically dead."

S: Why is there such a great discrepancy between the wonderful near-death experiences reported and the traumatic experiences of the people you've talked about?

MATTHEW: The glowing accounts in books come *from* people who are there on Earth, and the report I've given you is *about* people who are NOT. The physical dying process IS traumatic when the circumstances are violent, but obviously, this can't be reported on Earth by anyone who has experienced it! I must emphasize again that we're not talking about the transition from Earth life to this realm, which is NOT at all frightening, but about the traumatizing circumstances *prior* to physical death.

Mother, to thoroughly explain the difference, I need to describe the process of what you call "near-death experience." The experience of a severe physical shock is met with a correspondingly severe experience in spirit. That jolting of the etheric body, but not a total disconnection from the physical body, is the signal to the soul that it has the ability to leave the physical state and travel to the realm where it knows it has been before. Not always does the person have memory of previous visits here in dream state or in supraconscious moments, but there are those unique connections of the spirit that call forth this journey of the etheric body. The souls who make this journey have that near-death experience.

I have told you we know about the imminent arrivals by their distinctive and unmistakable energy blip identification mark. That same recognition is true of people in near-death experiencing. When their energy stream taps into the universal wavelengths, those who recognize it through love bonding respond instantly. That's why family members or friends in this realm and angels or other spirits are waiting for them.

People in near-death experiences don't enter by way of our welcoming and hospital stations. They are greeted at a special portal where the atmosphere is custom-created in accordance with their ideas of Heaven. We know what to manifest because the individual's universal record is made available so that all aspects of the visit can have maximum benefit. So, however at variance with what actually is here, the individuals' belief systems decree what they will see during the short visit. That expectation may include the appearance of the founder of their religion. If so, it is achieved by holographic representation, and the Christed energy of this realm emanates the love that these visitors may attribute to that founder.

True, souls who make transition also are treated to their envisioned Heaven upon entry, but that is a strategy for delicately introducing them into residency, and it's a temporary illusion. The personalized Heavens for people with near-death experiences remain throughout their short stay to avoid presenting an actuality that could be disturbing to their psyches, which will not have time to adjust to the truth of this realm. The more highly spiritually evolved the visiting soul, the more factually Nirvana is presented.

Since there is no need for medical treatment or explanation of all that the realm offers residents, there are only the joyous reunion aspects during the visit.

The visiting souls are completely aware of all they have left on the Earth plane, including the reason for their temporary release from physical body, and they are just as aware of all that is happening here. They are excited about seeing family members and friends, whom they talk with both telepathically and in speech.

Upon return to Earth, often a visitor remembers a controversy regarding whether he may or may not—that also can be "should" or "should not"—remain here. The decision to stay or return is solely that person's, and ALWAYS it has to do with provisions of his pre-birth agreement. Most of you would have a difficult time dealing with something as unknown as a pre-birth agreement, so the discussions here are not remembered accurately, but rather are put into the context of the belief system within the person's psyche. His memories of the controversy are converted by his usual mental processes into issues he can easily relate to on Earth. Thus his "reason" for returning may be remembered as a child's or spouse's or parent's need for care, or a desire to complete important personal or business affairs. Sometimes a visitor is eager to go back and make amends for what he realizes during his visit was wrongful treatment of others, and even though he won't remember any discussions of that sort, the desire remains once back on Earth and he acts upon that.

The decision to return is not always without influence from others. Council members, the guardian angel, or family members and friends who wish to help the visitor understand the seriousness of choosing to curtail major agreement provisions present cogent arguments against his remaining if he hasn't fulfilled those provisions. Those who see the larger picture of his lifetime mission advise so warmly and lovingly that usually he willingly returns to Earth. But as I said, once back there, those discussions are totally lost to his conscious memory.

S: Why can't they remember their experiences as they really happened?

MATTHEW: Once back in the third density of Earth they simply are not capable of awareness beyond their physical realities. Even though their dramatic and impressive spiritual experiences here impart some memory or interpretation intact, the full scope of what happened is forgotten in the density of their bodies.

What determines whether experiences will be remembered clearly, partially, incorrectly, or not at all, is not left up to chance. It's according to the laws of physics. It is the conversations, the scenes, the sense of timing that aren't remembered accurately. Those aspects are *mental* and require a similar mechanism for authentic memory. In this realm the visitor is operating within our fourth density in all ways. Returning to Earth is a return to third density faculties, which are incapable of comprehending at fourth density level. There simply cannot be accuracy when mental faculties are downloaded from fourth to third density, thus the heavier density of flesh traps the experiences, and the exactness of what happened is lost to the conscious memory.

What *is* retained is the sensation of love, the brightness of the light, the feelings of bonding and the desire to be in this familiar place. Those are never lost or distorted because they are faculties of the *soul,* not mental processes dependent upon the operation of the third-density brain or the psyche. The soul-level assimilation of the sensations is not distorted, therefore the *feelings* attached to the visit remain totally accurate.

S: How can those visitors be convinced that what they remember isn't exactly what they experienced?

MATTHEW: If you're asking for proof of the actual happenings, I don't know how that could be provided during the person's Earth lifetime because the only proof is here. The visit is recorded in his lifeprint in the Akashic Records exactly as it happened as well as how he remembered it, and both versions will be part of the life review process. Also, the people who talked with him will accurately remember what transpired, and when those same souls meet after that person's transition, they can attest to the actual happenings. But the ultimate proof is this: After transition, eventually he will have totally clear and complete memory of that brief visit and also the knowledge that his memories after returning to Earth were faulty. No other confirming source will be necessary.

S: But still, those people don't know the truth during the rest of their life here.

MATTHEW: Is that necessary, Mother? Isn't it enough for them to cherish the memories they have of their wondrous experience? Their sensations are valid, their feelings about those sensations are vital, and the experiences themselves bring wisdom essential for the individuals' spiritual growth.

S: You're right, Matthew. Is a person who wants to stay there ever permitted to do that?

MATTHEW: Yes, that can happen. Amendments to the pre-birth agreement can be made during the visit. If most of the provisions have been fulfilled and divine grace allows foregoing the remainder, then the physical body of that person simply dies and the soul in its etheric body stays here.

S: Is the sensation of being pulled through a dark tunnel toward a bright light the same for people making transition as it is for those in near-death experiences?

MATTHEW: I don't know. I didn't have a near-death experience so I don't have a personal comparison, and I haven't talked with anyone who has, at least not that I was aware of. But I suspect that there would be some difference in the sensation. In near-death experiencing the temporary parting of the physical and etheric bodies is not a complete disconnection, whereas the etheric body permanently leaves the physical body of the transitioning soul. The closeness of the two bodies cannot be underestimated. In either transition or visit, that lightning-fast journey never is difficult or frightening because of the transitional light energy.

S: Is a near-death experience a provision of a pre-birth agreement? And what is the ultimate value of the experience?

MATTHEW: It's not necessarily a provision, but it is related to the agreement. It is a dramatically influential occurrence, and rarely do those people who experience it return to their exact previous style of living. When the experience is called for in a pre-birth agreement, it is the same as with all other karmic lessons—for specific learning. When the experience is not a provision, then it's seen by the spirit helpers as a necessary stimulus to get the soul level behavior back on the lifetime track chosen in the agreement.

As for ultimate value, the profoundness of the experience heightens the person's awareness of his soul connection with God.

PRE-BIRTH AGREEMENTS, KARMA

S: Please tell me how pre-birth agreements are made.

MATTHEW: The agreements are contracts entered into at soul level by all members of a family and other primary relationships in the lifetimes of everyone agreeing to be born into the shared experiencing. Both genetic and environmental influences are taken into account when the selection of parents takes place, as these are the foundations for the soul's chosen lessons.

As an example, not only did I choose you as my mother and choose my father, but you and he and all my siblings agreed to experience your lives as my family. All of the other people dear to us, as well as those whose influences were essential for our chosen learning, also agreed to participate. You can see the complexity in matching up just these souls, but the agreement process didn't start even at that point when I chose my lifetime lessons. You chose your parents to experience your own selected growing and learning so you could fulfill the agreement provisions as their daughter as well as wife and mother in our family. Your parents chose their parents for the same reasons, and so on and so on throughout all the generations of ancestral lineage.

S: That much matching up of people is way beyond me, Matthew.

MATTHEW: It would be for almost everyone there, Mother. The matching up is through reviewing lifeprints in the Akashic Records. The universal law of continuum simultaneously accommodates past, present and future awareness of a situation. That alone is incomprehensible to you, because the linear time structure devised on Earth can't be applied.

I think I can best explain this agreement process and purpose if I continue using our family as an example. The six of us have been together many times, but more often only some of us have shared Earth and some intergalactic placement lifetimes. Repeated lifetimes with the same or most of the same principal souls—or, a soul cluster—isn't essential, but it is most usual because of the strengthened bonding and the karma being incurred and resolved within the group.

You and my father had completed karmic lessons in several lifetimes as mates, and you wanted to have a family again. However, you had clean karmic slates with each other, so both of you selected lessons to be completed from other relationships, and you did achieve the experiencing needed to fulfill those.

S: Those other relationships must have incurred a lot of bad karma! Actually—Matthew, exactly what is karma?

MATTHEW: Mother, I know the terms "good" or "bad" karma are commonly used to attribute experiences to some nebulous cause beyond one's knowing, or justify one's own or another's behavior, or achieve a measure of satisfaction that someone who isn't punished on Earth for foul deeds will "get his" in another lifetime. But there's no such thing as either "good" or "bad" karma. Karma is neither a punishment nor a reward, it is simply the law of the universe regarding cause and effect.

The objective of all soul learning is *balance,* and karma is the provision of the lessons a soul has selected to bring its experiencing into balance. Lifetimes are chosen based upon

conditions and events that will supply the missing experiences for the eventual balancing of the soul's cumulative
lifetime experiences. Not only pleasant lessons can be
chosen or the soul cannot grow beyond that point. Some
lessons are very difficult, but the soul is only experiencing the "other side of the coin," and it grows spiritually
by thoroughly learning the karmic lessons it selected for
that lifetime.

S: *Thank you for explaining that. Karma is quite different from what I thought, just people's isolated personal
struggles.*

MATTHEW: Here's an example of why it's not that.
There was another vital reason you and my father chose
at soul level to marry even knowing that for the most part,
you would not enjoy the union. The four of us children
needed the environment that would naturally develop from
our parents' stressful life together. The tension and dissen-
sion resulted in our need to form our own emotional stability and alliances with each other. You and my father provided
exactly the environment you had agreed to so that we children could learn the lessons we individually had chosen.

S: *Well, that's quite an illuminating perspective of all
we went through! Can someone request a change to the
agreement?*

MATTHEW: Yes, that can be done. Although agreements are designed to be honored by all participants for the
lifetime of the agreement, a soul may petition for an alteration in circumstances of utmost seriousness. For instance, a request may be for physical death prior to his

soul contract as a means to relieve prolonged physical, mental or emotional suffering. If the request is granted, it may be on the basis that the soul had suffered sufficiently for lesson completion or that part of the lesson could be awarded and the remainder incurred in another lifetime.

S: How is a change requested?

MATTHEW: A petition is submitted by the soul to our Council. The members consider all pertinent circumstances and the different experiencing for all affected souls if the request is granted. If the Council deems the request worthy, it's passed on at soul level to the other principals in the original plan. Obviously, when one life is changed significantly, all others within the parameters of the agreement are affected accordingly, so all must be in agreement once again. If all principals do agree, by divine grace the petition is granted.

An external situation also may be grounds for submitting a petition. If circumstances outside the agreement interrupted the chosen lessons, the soul may request an adjustment that will bring circumstances back into line or give relief from the adverse consequences of the interruption.

This is a unique time in Earth history, Mother. What has happened on a routine basis for eons is changing very rapidly in this time of preparation for a major transition of Earth. Agreements are far more flexible now than formerly to give opportunity for accelerated learning in encapsulated form rather than lifetime form. As light energy is beamed more and more heavily and steadily into Earth's atmosphere to lift the density, those on the lighted path are accelerated in their direction. Those on the dark path are as well, so it's harder now for those beings captured in dense energy to escape its headway.

AKASHIC RECORDS, LIFEPRINT REVIEW

S: I don't understand exactly what Akashic Records and lifeprints are or how they operate.

MATTHEW: Akashic Records contain complete, accurate, trustworthy accounts of all universe-wide happenings within eternity and All That Is. Lifeprints, which are as unique as your fingerprints and more impervious to alteration, form each soul's record, and each lifeprint is a separate file in the Akashic Records.

A lifeprint is like a lifelong movie, omitting not a single aspect or instant. The information it contains, which automatically and indelibly is registered in energy form, is every thought, every action, and the consequences of every action throughout the lifetime of the person. Every action is registered as the deed itself plus the intent and all feelings associated with it. Not only are the person's feelings about every action and its results recorded, but the feelings of all the people whose lives were affected by those actions.

After the soul has recovered stability from the previous lifetime and is nourished spiritually and psychically, it is completely aware of its cumulative soul. It is this cumulative soul, with its collective wisdom and knowledge and spiritual growth of all personage lifetimes, that reviews the lifeprint. The reviewing process is *felt* exactly as those feelings were experienced not only by the person, but all the people who were affected by his every action. So you can see that it is quite an experience!

The cumulative soul's judgment of its previous lifetime is the ONLY judgment of it. You have heard that only God is your judge and you also have heard that even God does not judge. Either way, this refers to the lifeprint review. Because we all are fragments of God and therefore inextricably connected, it is accurate to say that only God, in each personage, judges. And it is just as accurate to say that He doesn't judge at all, because only the cumulative soul whose last personage lifetime is under review judges it.

In this intimate review the soul evaluates how well it learned the lessons presented during the previous lifetime. A lax assessment of which lessons were thoroughly learned and which were not may be addressed by the Council or other highly evolved beings whose recommendations are meant to assist that soul's preparation for the next incarnation. The lifeprint review also identifies lessons remaining, thus enabling the soul to choose those it wishes to experience in its next lifetime. This entails examining karmic connections and selecting a family to be born into for the genetic and beginning environmental influences.

There is another aspect of the lifeprint records that is relevant when the soul discusses the next life and lessons with advisers: Lifeprints are not cast in marble by the physical death of the individual. Their elastic form permits alteration of the record if another soul interfered with the soul's chosen experiencing. If that interference seriously diverted the soul from its chosen pathway, by divine grace the lifeprint may be altered to reflect that. The affected soul may incur "positive" karma or may pass altogether if remaining lessons do not include that unplanned experiencing. The soul who caused the diversion incurs "negative" karma, which is registered in his lifeprint.

S: With so many entries, how can the lifeprint be safe-guarded from either honest error or tampering?

MATTHEW: The lifeprint's continuous and automatic updating throughout each lifetime of the soul is done only by that soul. Since the record is energy registrations entered simultaneously with the soul's every thought, action and feeling, there simply is no room for error. If a soul even thought about manipulating entries to its favor, that unscrupulous thought also would be registered.

The energy of the lifeprint is compatible *only* with its soul's energy, and therefore it can be changed only by an infusion of identical energy. If tampering were attempted, a signal would alert the record keepers, and the would-be infiltrator would be recognized through his own unique energy coding. With this foolproof safeguard system, no soul would be so foolish as to try to alter another's lifeprint.

Furthermore, lifeprints cannot be accessed easily for examination, and never merely out of curiosity. For the sanctity of each soul's experiences, permission to enter frivolously is denied by means of that energy encoding. As a transition assister I have valid reason for entering the records of the souls whose lifetime information I need for maximum help to them. The needs of each arrival I assist and my function carry reciprocal energy that constitutes his implied consent to my entering his record, and our energy meshing is my automatic access code to it.

Part of the intergalactic warring has been to gain dominance over the records, for either annihilation or to establish a new coding system that would allow the victors to manipulate the records. Ashtar is the oversoul energy commanding the forces that operate and protect the records. I cannot imagine the mechanics involved in their responsibility for an awesome mass of energy in its countless forms, all the way from each soul's record up to the coalescence of All That Is.

COUNCIL OF NIRVANA

S: I know the Council is your governing body, but I don't know how they're chosen for their positions or exactly what they do.

MATTHEW: I will tell you, Mother. Only the most honored and wisest souls are considered for Council membership. Their backgrounds vary, with wisdom rather than professional and academic knowledge being the major criterion for the position. In most cases, the members have had many embodiments on Earth, but their lifetimes are by no means confined to Earth experiencing.

The membership is representative of male, female and androgynous souls. It includes newcomers with great wisdom and knowledge, masters who have chosen to remain in this realm even though their spiritual evolvement could elevate them several notches beyond Nirvana, and a grand master who is petitioned as needed. The grand master is not in residence nor is it in body. This powerful energy is transient throughout this solar system and into planetary systems most closely associated with the development of Earth civilization, such as Lyra, Sirius and the Pleiades.

The full Council may number over a hundred, but not all members would be present except when the gravest of matters must be addressed. Generally ten are in attendance at regular sessions as that number usually can handle all requests without delay, and never less than six are available. During times of great activity that require the attention of the Council elsewhere, such as mass death episodes on Earth, there are no regular sessions. However, always some member is available for consultation, and more can be assembled within an instant for emergencies.

Sessions are held in a fine but not ornate marble building that does justice to the Council's high level of assistance and responsibility. Due to its use, the building is radiant with the essence of the Christed light, and the light energy of the Council members adds to that glistening essence. Their presence amplifies the light intensity of the realm wherever they are.

Here it truly is the will of the masses that governs and not the will of the leaders if there is conflict between any leader and the residents. It is based upon a republic foundation, with the advantage that a selection or recall can be made quickly. The members are chosen by a widespread vote of confidence that elevates the selected individuals into Council positions. A recall could happen in the same way. The undercurrent of dissatisfaction grows to a potent thought form base and the member is bound by the energy to relinquish the position. However, the intentions of self-serving souls will not accomplish this selection or replacement process, so a handful of heavily Earth-influenced newcomers cannot dislodge a Council member.

Everything affecting this realm or our beloved souls on Earth would fall under the province of the Council. With the exception of Earth, they interface with governing agencies of all realms that have any impact upon us. The Council's interaction on Earth is with extraterrestrial entities from the angelic and spirit realms and the human and suprahuman civilizations who are assisting your planet as light workers during this time of universal changes.

The Council keeps abreast of all that is happening throughout the universe. To be certain they are totally current on latest developments or every aspect of a specific issue, they research all available resource material and consult authorities in other realms who have expertise on the subject.

In addition to being senior management, they are our chief advisers on all matters of critical nature to the realm, and of individual need as well. To make an appointment with the Council, most often one simply approaches a doorway soul. That soul doesn't prohibit entry but only maintains order if there is a great rush of people wanting to meet with the members. It isn't uncommon for a requester to be ushered into the chambers immediately when he has a relatively minor matter that can be handled by only one member. If research is required, then a second meeting is held.

When someone needs advice of Council but the reason isn't urgent, an appointment will be scheduled for sufficient time and for privacy, if desired. Members not only offer the advice requested, but also educate the requester fully on the pertinent topic to expand that soul's knowledge. There is no limit to the number of times one may approach the Council.

S: Do they appear in body?

MATTHEW: Yes, and I see your further question, Mother—what do they wear? They wear white robes with gold cord sashes. Their attire wouldn't distinguish them from anyone else here, but there is no mistaking their light essence that denotes their distinctive wisdom, knowledge and position.

S: Matthew, I'm interested in what people wear so I can visualize every possible aspect of that place! Have you ever met with any Council members?

MATTHEW: OK, Mother, it's just that I still don't share your interest in clothes. Yes, I've met with the Council members on many occasions. Most recently I appeared before the full Council immediately after a break in my transmission to you because it was an urgent matter that could have affected the entire realm. My suspicion was right—it was a rent in our protective shield that enabled the base spirits to invade our sitting. As I've mentioned, that is a very rare occurrence, and instant attention to it was imperative.

On another recent occasion my meeting concerned two of your former colleagues. I felt my scope of information was insufficient to advise you, so I extended your inquiry to a higher source who had information I didn't, a Council member who is especially cognizant of inner plane happenings as related to Earth individuals. He enlightened me about their activities and their dangerous journey for this Earth lifetime as well as their ongoing struggles on the inner planes, and he cautioned against your remaining involved. He was the source of the advice I passed on to you. That was not invading your privacy or interfering in your life by him or me, because you had asked me what you should do. It was your decision to heed or ignore the warning.

Also I have offered suggestions which the Council has implemented. Always suggestions are offered freely with only the contribution itself and the warm but quiet courtesy of appreciation from the Council as one's reward. We don't have the public recognition or ceremony here that often accompanies an unusual service on Earth. What we do have is the understanding that spiritual growth is automatically sharing glimmers or bursts of awareness.

REMEMBERING

S: What kind of suggestions would you or anyone else offer the Council? From all you've told me about Nirvana, everything seems to be going perfectly, so why would any changes be necessary?

MATTHEW: Mother, you still are tied to your concept of a utopian Heaven, and by comparison to other placements, that isn't an unreasonable impression of our world. But it is a fallacy that perfection reigns here! *You are mortal and may err. I am in Heaven and I may not.* Well, the frail human condition remains here long enough so that "to err is human" still applies. Every soul here is in a growth mode, and we are not without aspects needing correction, improvement, clarification, enlightenment.

I know I've referred many times to "learning" and "lessons" both here and on Earth, but actually, Mother, *nothing* has to be "learned." Everything that IS, we already KNOW at soul level. As we are inseparable from God and Creator, so we are inseparable from the universal mind. *It is consciously remembering all we know that is the journey through all our lifetimes.*

Until every soul has *earned* its way back to the light with memory of all experiencing intact, nowhere in this universe can be considered the Heaven of religions or the Utopia of fable. It is the completeness of experiencing and the earned return to Creator that is the culmination of the promise of perfection in eternity. The ongoing fulfillment of that eternal life is in the growth journey of the soul.

Mother, I know you sometimes wonder if it really matters if people there don't know all the facets of this realm, that it's enough that it fits some of the Heaven, hell, and purgatory ideas of some religions, the reincarnation and karma of others, and the eternal life of most. Maybe it doesn't matter if not every detail of life here is known there, but shouldn't the *essential* TRUTH of Nirvana be known?

The answer to that can only be "YES!" How else can the people of Earth know the vital need for emotional balance and nonjudgment of others, or realize their capacity for negative or positive influence on a *universal* scale? How else can they grow in spiritual awareness and glory for the duration of their life there and prepare knowledgeably, joyously, for their next lifetime here?

GLOSSARY

Akashic records. Universal recording and storage system of all souls' experiencing in all lifetimes.

Androgyny. Balanced state of male and female energies.

Angelic realms. Placements of pure love and light closest to Creator.

Angels. Collective beings of light manifested by archangels in co-creation with Creator.

Archangels. First beings created by Creator.

Aspect. Individuated part of a cumulative soul; also called personage, soul fragment, God spark.

Balance. Goal and epitome of all experiencing.

Christ. State of being one with God.

Christed light. Manifestation of Creator's love, constantly available to all beings for soul evolvement and protection from dark forces.

Co-creation. Process or product of souls manifesting in conjunction with Creator.

Cosmos. Composite of all universes created by Creator; sometimes used interchangeably with "universe" in reference to our universe.

Creator. Supreme being of the cosmos; also referred to as Totality, Oneness, All That Is, I AM, etc.; sometimes used interchangeably with "God" to denote supreme being of our universe.

Cumulative soul. Ever-expanding composite of all experiencing in all lifetimes of its individual personages.

Dark forces. Powers originating in deepest antiquity whose experiencing choices eventually eliminated all light except a spark at their soul level; foes of light beings and of the light itself; evil.

Density. In accordance with universal laws, dimensions of soul experiencing and spiritual evolvement descending from the pure light and love of Creator into total spiritual darkness.

Energy. Basis of all life throughout the cosmos.

Energy attachments. Positive or negative interpretations given the effects of any energy motion.

Etheric body. Body used in spirit realms.

Extraterrestrial. Any place beyond planet Earth; non-Earth civilizations.

Free will. Each soul's ability to choose and manifest lifetime experiencing.

God. One name given the supreme being of our universe, and as such, possessing all power, wisdom and knowledge of Creator.

Guardian angel. Primary celestial helper assigned to each person for spiritual guidance and physical protection.

Karma. Cause and effect of a soul exercising free will; basis for selecting subsequent lifetime experiencing.

Lifeprint. A soul's file in the Akashic Records; complete accounting of a soul's lifetime thoughts, feelings, actions and their consequences.

Light. Creator's wisdom, love and the power of love manifested in energy form.

Lost souls. Souls whose free will choices led to entrenchment in the basest density placement.

Manifestation. Process or product of co-creating with Creator; the inherent ability and indivisible aspect of free will.

Mission. Primary purpose of each lifetime, selected for spiritual growth by the soul prior to birth of its personage.

4 fourfourfour4fourfour 444four44four4four44four4444444four4444four4444four4444four4444four44four4444four4four4four4four444four4four4four4four4four4four4four4four4444four4four4four4four4four4four4four4four4four4four4four4four4four4four4four4four4four4four4four4four4four4four4four4four4four4four4four44four4four4four4four4four4four4four4four4four4four4four4four4four4four4four4four4four4four4four4four4four4four4four4four4four4four4four4four4four4four4four4four4four4four4four4four4four4four4four4four4four4four4four4four4four4four4four4four4four4four4four4four4four4four4four4four4four4four4four4four4four

Negativity. In accordance with universal laws, the destructive forces initiated and expanded by dark thought forms.

Nirvana. Proper name of the realm we call Heaven.

Personage. Independent and inviolate essence of a soul experiencing an incarnate lifetime.

Placement. Realm composed of various related areas for specific experiencing.

Prayer. Direct communion with God through thoughts and feelings.

Pre-birth agreement. Soul level agreement made prior to incarnation by all primary souls participating in a shared lifetime.

Reincarnation. Return to a physical life after a discarnate life.

Reintegration. Through spiritual evolvement, the return of all souls to Creator.

Soul. Spiritual life force; inviolate essence of each individual's inextricable connection with God and all other life forms throughout the universe.

Spirit guides. Discarnate beings other than angels who are our unseen helpers.

Thought forms. Indelible and eternal energy substances produced by mental processes of all souls from the Beginning; the stuff of universal knowledge.

Transition. After death of the physical body, the soul's lightning-fast passage in etheric body to Nirvana.

Universal laws. Parameters within which all souls experience and to which all are subject; also called laws of God, laws of nature.

Universal mind. All knowledge in the universe; the total of all thought forms, available for accessing by any soul.

Universe. One of several such placements of incalculable size manifested by Creator and the angelic realms.

THE MATTHEW BOOKS

The Matthew Books continue with *Revelations for a New Era.*

The *Conversations with God* series answered all the most important questions of my life, but that led to a million new questions. *Revelations for a New Era* answered those; it is the 'how it works' of the new cosmology.
—**Zurina Susan Abdullah**, Malaysia

Revelations for a New Era provides—in plain language—a comprehensive, multidimensional, highly conscious and concise spiritual overview of the radical transformations occurring on planet Earth.

The astonishing scope and lucidity of the information transmitted by the disincarnate Matthew Ward to his earthbound mother Suzanne includes and corroborates almost every area of metaphysical enquiry. In view of recent paradigm-shaking events, this book is ESSENTIAL reading for anyone who urgently needs to understand our options at this critical juncture in our evolution.

I am heartened and relieved to know that such empowering esoteric knowledge is now easily available to the reading public.
—**Antares**, Malaysia

The Matthew Books can be ordered through **www.matthewbooks.com** or your favorite local or on-line bookstore.